The Strategy of
Soviet Imperialism

THE STRATEGY OF SOVIET IMPERIALISM

Expansion in Eurasia

MARTIN SICKER

PRAEGER

New York
Westport, Connecticut
London

Library of Congress Cataloging-in-Publication Data

Sicker, Martin.
   The strategy of Soviet imperialism.

   Bibliography: p.
   Includes index.
   1. Soviet Union—Foreign relations. I. Title.
DK66.S54   1988   327.47   87–25882
ISBN 0–275–92932–9

Library of Congress Catalog Card Number: 87–25882

ISBN: 0–275–92932–9

First published in 1988

Praeger Publishers, One Madison Avenue, New York, NY 10010
A division of Greenwood Press, Inc.

Printed in the United States of America

The paper used in this book complies with the
Permanent Paper Standard issued by the National
Information Standards Organization (Z39.48–1984).

10   9   8   7   6   5   4   3   2   1

This book is dedicated to
My in-laws
Joshua and Eugenie Fixman
May their memory serve as a blessing

Contents

The Strategy of
Soviet Imperialism

1 Introduction: Imperialism under Czars and Commissars

One of the aspects of Soviet strategic thinking that is particularly difficult for Western analysts to internalize concerns the element of time. In a vigorous democratic society, characterized by a free and almost completely uninhibited press and frequent elections where the fundamental issues of national policy are laid bare before the public, patience tends to be rare. There is a tendency to rush to judgment so that accomplishment can be shown before the next periodic public accounting. It is virtually inconceivable in such a society that policies and goals can be pursued persistently over long periods of time without showing tangible results. Thus, when considering Soviet policy and strategy, there is a tendency to approach the question from a Western perspective, that is, "If I were in the Kremlin, this is what I would do." Unfortunately, such mirror imaging is rarely accompanied by the critical recognition that the Soviets are in fact not the same as we are. Soviet political culture is vastly different from our own, as are the historical and geographical factors that contribute to its particular geopolitical orientation. In particular, the Soviet approach to the problem of time reflects a perspective truly alien to Western political experience. As George F. Kennan observed a generation ago,

We have seen that the Kremlin is under no ideological compulsion to accomplish its purposes in a hurry . . . The very teachings of Lenin himself require great caution and flexibility in the pursuit of Communist purposes. Again, these precepts are fortified by the lessons of Russian history: of centuries of obscure battles between nomadic forces over the stretches of a vast unfortified plain. Here caution, circumspection, flexibility and deception are the valuable qualities; and their value finds natural appreciation in the Russian or the oriental mind. Thus the Kremlin has no compunction about retreating in the face of superior force. And being under the compulsion of no timetable, it does not get panicky under the necessity for such retreat. Its political action is a fluid stream which moves constantly, wherever it is permitted to move, toward a given goal. Its main concern is to make sure that it has filled every nook and cranny available to it in the basin of world power. But if it finds unassailable barriers in its path, it accepts these philosophically and accommodates itself to them. The main thing is that there should always be pressure, unceasing constant pressure, toward the desired goal.[1]

From a historical perspective, the pattern of Russian expansion is coherent and has contributed greatly to the extraordinary growth of the Russian and Soviet empires over the last 400 years. The essential characteristics of this pattern may be readily discerned through even a cursory examination of Russian imperial history and that of the successor Soviet state. One pervasive feature of this pattern is the tendency to probe in several directions of interest, but ultimately to move inexorably along the path of least resistance.[2] Indeed, as stated most pointedly by Lord Palmerston in 1853, "the policy and practise of the Russian Government has always been to push forward its encroachments as fast and as far as the apathy or want of firmness of other governments would allow it to go; but always to stop and retire when it was met with decided resistance, and then to wait for the next favourable opportunity."[3]

A second typical feature has been the tendency to expand almost exclusively, at least until contemporary times, along interior lines of communication. That is, expansion was pursued from contiguous territories that were already under control, so that the lines of communication, between the military forces and colonial settlers at the front of the salient and their sources of supply and reinforcement to the rear, were secure against the threat of interdiction. A third prominent characteristic has been the extensive use of deception, subversion, and intimidation as instruments to facilitate the imperial advance. The significance of these factors becomes evident when one considers the situation of czarist Russia at the end of the sixteenth century, concentrated in a sizable but nonetheless relatively small enclave centered on Moscow, and once again four centuries later.

For some 400 years, first under the czars and later under its commissars, Russia has pursued an unrelenting policy of imperialism. Disregarding the contemporary appropriation of the term by the communist world as a pejorative applied solely and most often improperly to the world's democracies, it is the Soviet Union that is today's major imperialist power. As Hans J. Morgenthau once wrote, "a nation whose foreign policy aims at acquiring more power than it actually has through expansion of its power beyond its frontiers, whose foreign policy, in other words, seeks a favorable change in power status, pursues a policy of imperialism."[4] That is, imperialism is "a policy which aims at the overthrow of the status quo, at a reversal of the power relations between two or more nations."[5]

Until the immediate post–World War II period, Soviet imperialist policy was characterized primarily by territorial aggrandizement and colonization or Russification. Since then, it has taken on other newer and more sophisticated forms involving satellite, client, and other types of interstate relationship. Thus, though contemporary Soviet expansionism may no longer involve territorial annexation and colonization, it remains imperialist nonetheless. The Soviet Union of today continues its long-standing commitment to the extension of its control and influence across the globe generally, and in the Eastern Hemisphere in particular. Its policies thus reflect the continuity, although perhaps on a scale surpassing that of its predecessors, of Russian imperialist ambition into the present era.

Bearing in mind this nexus between czarist and Soviet imperialism, it is of particular interest to recall the description of the earlier form of Russian expansionism provided in the letter written by Karl Marx on May 31, 1853 to the *New York Tribune* and published in its pages on June 14, 1853. The letter directs the reader's attention to Russia's exceptional record of destroying those nations that it was purportedly committed to protect.

Mankind will not forget that Russia was the PROTECTOR of Poland, the PROTECTOR of the Crimea, the PROTECTOR of Courland, the PROTECTOR of Georgia, Mingrelia, the Circassian and Caucasian tribes. And now Russia, the PROTECTOR of Turkey! As to Russia's antipathy against aggrandizement,

I allege the following facts from a mass of the acquisitions of Russia since Peter the Great.

The Russian frontier has advanced:

Towards Berlin, Dresden and Vienna, about	700 miles
Towards Constantinople	500 miles
Towards Stockholm	630 miles
Towards Teheran	1,000 miles

Russian acquisitions from Sweden are greater than what remains of that kingdom; from Poland, nearly equal to the Austrian Empire; from Turkey in Europe, greater than Prussia (exclusive of the Rhenish Provinces); from Turkey in Asia, as large as the whole dominion of Germany proper; from Persia, equal to England; from Tartary, to an extent as large as European Turkey, Greece, Italy, and Spain, taken together. The total acquisitions of Russia during the last sixty years are equal in extent and importance to the whole world empire she had in Europe before that time.[6]

As the czarist empire expanded, its intrinsic character effectively precluded Russia from following the path of development that led to the rise of the modern nation-states of Europe and America. The czarist empire was different in one critical respect from the British, French, Dutch, and Portuguese empires. The holdings of these empires were primarily abroad and distant from the homeland. It was thus possible for these states to undergo the transition to an integral nation-state while maintaining a remote colonial empire. By contrast, the Russian empire was the only one whose imperial holdings were contiguous to Russia itself. While the Russians constituted the majority in the czarist state, the pattern of annexations pursued by the czars transformed Russia into a conglomerate composed of many distinct national entities that were unassimilable into a coherent nation-state. Eventually, as was the case with all empires in modern history, pressures began to build that threatened to tear apart the fabric of this multinational colossus. However, the fact of the physical contiguity of the empire on the Eurasian land mass created the unprecedented problems of determining what was and what was not intrinsic to Russia, and of maintaining the state itself intact.

The disruptions and dislocations caused by World War I, compounded by the civil strife that was engendered by the Bolshevik Revolution that followed, unleashed a host of latent nationalisms that sought expression through self-determination. Separatist movements quickly arose in Byelorussia, Finland, Estonia, Latvia, Lithuania, the Ukraine, Georgia, Armenia, and Turkestan. Lenin himself initially recognized the legitimacy of their aspirations, even if it meant the possible dissolution of large segments of the Russian state. However, once ensconced in the Kremlin, he and his colleagues promptly took steps to prevent the breakup of the new Soviet-controlled empire. To deal with the problem of maintaining the integrity of the multinational state, the Soviet leaders adopted a novel approach.

The ideology that Lenin and his heirs and disciples transformed into the civil religion of the Soviet state subordinated all national distinctions to the transnational struggle of the classes. Class cut directly across the lines of nationality. The notion of the transnational unity of the proletariat as the progressive leading class was to become the organizing principle of the new Soviet empire. Under such a concept, Lenin could be consistent in continuing to maintain that all peoples had an inherent right to national self-determination; however, proletarian solidarity demanded that the exercise of that right had to be subordinated to the higher needs of the transnational class struggle. For the sake of this struggle, it was imperative that the empire be kept intact.

The new ruling class, later to become known as the *nomenklatura*, proclaimed at the time of the creation of the Soviet state that it was going to make a complete break with the imperialist and colonialist policies of czarist Russia, but instead it stubbornly continued to pursue the traditional expansionism of the czars.[7] Notwithstanding their ritual invocations of the highest ideals of Marxism as interpreted by Lenin, it was not long before they recognized that the only plausible justification for their arrogation of the power, influence, and affluence of the czarist regime that had recently been overthrown and replaced was the necessity for the ongoing pursuit of the historic imperialist pattern of "external expansion, the establishment of its rule over foreign countries and the exploitation of their wealth."[8] This was being done, of course, in the name of the "revolution" that was to be promoted everywhere in the ultimate interests of the international proletariat, who were to be liberated in the process.

For the Kremlin, the period between the two world wars was devoted largely to consolidating the Soviet Union and experimenting with the exportation of the revolution beyond the contiguous borders of the empire. With the end of World War II, the Soviet Union went on an imperialist rampage that quickly reintegrated the Baltic states into the empire and reduced East Germany, Poland, Czechoslovakia, Hungary, Romania, Bulgaria, and Mongolia to a modern form of vassalage. They became Soviet satellites. Moscow established close ties to the communist regimes of North Korea and Vietnam. It reached across the seas to the Western Hemisphere, where Cuba has long been a Soviet dependency, and where Nicaragua is on its way to becoming one as well. It has also brought within its embrace the Marxist states of Afghanistan, Angola, Ethiopia, Mozambique, and South Yemen and has extended its influence over numerous other countries in the Third World.

Parallel to the new wave of Soviet expansionism, the Kremlin has evolved a theory of empire that in its full articulation, in what has become known in the West as the Brezhnev Doctrine, poses a serious challenge to the foundations of international law and the current practice of interstate relations. This doctrine finds its roots in the Marxist-Leninist concept of "proletarian internationalism."

At the Second World Congress of the Communist International (Comintern) in 1920, Lenin defined proletarian internationalism as requiring that the interests of the class struggle in any single country be subordinated to the broader interests of the international proletariat in its struggle with capitalism. The Communist Party of the Soviet Union (CPSU) was presumed to be the vanguard of the world communist movement and, consequently, the arbiter of the aims, needs, and priorities of proletarian internationalism. At the Comintern's Fifth World Congress in 1925, it was further resolved that the experiences of the CPSU, to the extent that they had applicability outside the Soviet Union, could be mandated as guidelines for the various communist parties, if deemed necessary. The CPSU, in the interests of proletarian internationalism, was to set the standards and the pace by which the development of the communist universe was to be regulated.

In 1943, for tactical reasons, Stalin abolished the Comintern and promulgated the new theory of "different roads to socialism." This effectively permitted the Communist parties, which had been under Moscow's direct control through the Comintern, to cooperate with other "progressive" elements in their respective countries. This tactic ultimately facilitated the communist seizure of power and the establishment of people's democracies in Eastern Europe and Asia after the end of the war in 1945. The tactic backfired in the cases of Mao's China and Tito's Yugoslavia, where the theory of "different roads to socialism" was taken seriously, and where Moscow's attempts to dictate policy were rejected. Chastened by the loss of control over these two communist countries, Stalin soon discarded the theory and moved with determination to assert Soviet hegemony over the people's democracies of Eastern Europe on the basis of the earlier doctrine of proletarian internationalism. Moscow no longer sought to incorporate the Eastern European countries into the Soviet Union. Soviet imperialism now took new forms. The essence of Stalin's strategy was to secure his geopolitical objectives by controlling a ring of vassal states, nominally sovereign but subject to the discipline of proletarian internationalism, as a buffer zone to provide strategic depth for the Soviet Union and forward positions for power projection toward Western Europe.

Stalin's iron grip on the satellite states proved to be very costly and inefficient. His successors sought to reaffirm Soviet control through cooperative measures rather than coercion. On May 14, 1955 a treaty of "friendship, cooperation, and mutual aid" (the Warsaw Pact) was signed between the Soviet Union and Poland, Romania, Czechoslovakia, East Germany, Hungary, Bulgaria, and Albania. The key provisions of this treaty were Article 5, which placed the armed forces of all the signatories under a single command, which in practice is always Soviet; and Article 7, which made it clear that the signatories were precluded from entering into any other alliance. This not only was a clear infringement of the sovereignty of the signatory states but also made it evident that they were an integral part of the Soviet system of states, the Soviet empire. Once this arrangement was put in place, the new Soviet leaders reintroduced the theory of "different roads to socialism," which was given the imprimatur of the CPSU at its XX Party Congress in February 1956. However, in his commentary on the "different roads" theory, chief party theoretician Mikhail Suslov offered an interpretation of the theory within the context of proletarian internationalism that was to prove to be of critical importance in the years ahead. Suslov maintained that the transition to a communist system of rule is irreversible and any attempt to restore the *status quo ante* is to be met and opposed with organized resistance.[9] The implications of this interpretation became understood later that same year.

In October 1956 the Soviets were confronted, for the first time, by the prospect of a defection of a member of the international "socialist community." On October 22, Hungarian students set forth a sixteen-point program for reform of the Hungarian communist state, which included, most notably, the withdrawal of the Soviet forces stationed in the country in accordance with the Warsaw Pact of 1955, a multiparty political system, and free elections. On October 30 the Soviets issued a statement pointing out the nature of the relationship between the Soviet Union and its communist allies. This statement, although somewhat ambiguous, nonetheless was clearly intended as a signal to Budapest that a reversion to a noncommunist system was unacceptable. It stated in part:

The Soviet government proceeds from the principle that the stationing of troops of another member state of the Warsaw Treaty takes place on the basis of an agreement between all its participants and not only of the agreement of that state on the territory of which, at its request, these troops are stationed or are planned to be stationed. . . . The defense of the socialist gains of people's democratic Hungary is today the chief and sacred obligation of the workers, peasants, and intellectuals, of all Hungarian working people. The Soviet government expresses confidence that the peoples of the socialist countries will not allow external and internal reactionary forces to shake the foundations of the people's democratic system, won and reinforced by the selfless struggle and labor of the workers, peasants, and intellectuals of each country.[10]

The intent of the message was apparently misunderstood by the Hungarian leadership. The first part, cited above, should have made clear that, notwithstanding the additional Soviet statement that Moscow was withdrawing its forces in order not to exacerbate the situation, the decision regarding the presence of Soviet troops in a Warsaw Pact country was not one that the host country could make unilaterally. The second part of the message clearly warned that Moscow expected "the peoples of the socialist countries" to protect the Marxist-Leninist revolution against encroachment. Nevertheless, on that same day, the government of Imre Nagy withdrew from the Warsaw Pact and terminated the single-party status of the Communist party.

The Kremlin decided on intervention. To provide a facade of legitimacy for the obvious forthcoming violation of Hungary's sovereignty, the Soviets helped Janos Kadar establish a new Hungarian Communist party the very next day and a new government on November 4. Kadar promptly and dutifully requested Soviet aid in suppressing the revolt and ousting the outlaw Nagy regime. Moscow was only too happy to assist a fraternal communist state, especially since this provided the after-the-fact fig leaf needed to cover the Soviet intervention, which had already started on October 31, five days earlier.

Ferenc A. Vali has observed: "It is, of course, erroneous to pretend that in October-November 1956 only the fate of Hungary was at stake. The Hungarian uprising was only one outward sign of the general unrest that existed throughout the satellite area. . . . The question was only superficially one of Hungary; in fact, it was a question of Soviet domination in East-Central Europe, and implicitly one of Soviet-Communist imperial power sustained or in demise."[11]

The Hungarian crisis thus provided the Soviet Union with a laboratory in which to test the limits of stress that the empire could bear. Eastern Europe had clearly been within the Soviet sphere of influence since 1945, but the relationship between the satellite states and the Soviet Union was still loosely defined. Now Moscow had promulgated and applied the rules by which that sphere was henceforth to be defined and governed. The CPSU was the preeminent organ of international socialism, and the Soviet Union could and would use its state power to preserve and regulate the socialist community of states. It would not permit the defection of any state from the new configuration of the Soviet empire. This was made abundantly clear by Nikita Khrushchev in his address to the Seventh Congress of the Hungarian Socialist Workers' Party on December 1, 1959, when he stated: "We must keep in mind that the attempt to bring about a falling out among the socialist countries, to weaken fraternal, friendly ties among them, is one of the forms of class struggle used by our adversary. It is for this reason that the immutable principles of proletarian internationalism are the supreme unalterable law of the international communist movement."[12]

The Hungarian experience also served to reinforce the Soviet *nomenklatura* and its policy of preserving the status quo in the Soviet Union. Milovan Djilas observed shortly after the suppression of the Hungarian revolt: "Had the Hungarian Revolution been saved from Soviet intervention, it would have been difficult indeed for Moscow to obscure its internal conflicts by means of foreign conquests and the 'world mission.' The Soviet system would soon have been confined to its own national boundaries, and there, too, the citizens would be forced to reflect on their position and their destiny. . . . Thus, new processes would begin in the Soviet Union, too."[13]

During the dozen years that followed the Hungarian affair, the Soviets became deeply engaged in ideological warfare with the two states that had managed to slip out of Stalin's grasp, Yugoslavia and China. Although Mao was strongly supportive of the Soviet intervention in Hungary, he, assisted by Tito, fought zealously to undercut Soviet predominance in the communist world. Consequently, the Kremlin found the time inexpedient to press the matter of Soviet hegemony. It was not long, however, before a new crisis in the Soviet empire compelled Moscow to reassert its position as the guardian of proletarian internationalism forcefully. Once again, it gave tangible demonstration of the thesis that a member state of the socialist community might theoretically have the right to secede from it, but the higher needs of proletarian internationalism would not countenance the exercise of that right.

This time the problem was in Czechoslovakia. The communist leadership of that country undertook to make changes in its system that proved to be unacceptable to the Soviet Union. As in the earlier case of Hungary, a warning was issued, and the failure by the Czech authorities to comply with Moscow's strictures soon resulted in the 1968 military intervention in Prague by the Soviet Union and several other members of the Warsaw Pact. This episode marked a significant milestone in the Soviet drive for undisputed hegemony in Eurasia. The immediate issue was the reform movement in Czechoslovakia, which sought, as characterized by the Czech leader Dubcek, to have "socialism with a human face." Czechoslovakia's reform movement was applauded by the leaders of Yugoslavia and Romania, who saw it as reinforcing their own deviations from Moscow's version of orthodox communism. In Moscow, however, the Czech initiative was seen as a direct challenge to Soviet hegemony in Eastern Europe and consequently a threat to the stability of the socialist community of states, that is, the Soviet empire.

On July 3, 1968, Brezhnev had declared that the Soviet Union could never be indifferent to "the fate of socialist construction in other countries, to the common cause of socialism and communism in the world."[14] On July 15 the Soviet Union, in conjunction with Poland, Hungary, Bulgaria, and East Germany, the states that would soon join in the intervention in Czechoslovakia, issued the *Warsaw Letter*, which depicted developments in Prague as a danger to the "common life interests" of other socialist countries. The letter went on to assert:

We cannot assent to hostile forces pushing your country off the path of socialism and creating the threat that Czechoslovakia may break away from the socialist commonwealth. This is no longer your affair alone. . . . It is the common affair of our countries, which have united in the Warsaw Pact to safeguard their independence, peace, and security in Europe and to place an insurmountable barrier in front of the schemes of imperialist forces, aggression, and revanche . . .

The frontiers of the socialist world have shifted to the center of Europe, to the Elbe and the Bohemian Forest. And never will we consent to allow these historic gains of socialism and the independence and security of all our peoples to be jeopardized. Never will we consent to allow imperialism, by peaceful or nonpeaceful means, from within or without, to make a breach in the socialist system and change the balance of power in Europe in its favor . . .

Our countries are bound to one another by treaties and agreements. These important mutual commitments of states and peoples are founded on a common desire to defend socialism and safeguard the collective security of the socialist countries. Our parties and peoples are entrusted with the historical responsibility of seeing that the revolutionary gains achieved are not forfeited.

Each of our parties bears a responsibility not only to its own working class and its own people but also to the international working class and the world communist movement and cannot evade the obligations deriving from this. Therefore we must have solidarity and unity in defense of the gains of socialism, our security, and the international positions of the entire socialist commonwealth.

This is why we believe that it is not only your task but ours too to deal a resolute rebuff to the anticommunist forces and to wage a resolute struggle for the preservation of the socialist system in Czechoslovakia.[15]

Again, as in the case of Hungary in 1956, Moscow's message was obviously not clearly understood. The Czechs apparently felt secure in pursuing their reform of the system, since they were proposing something rather different than was the case in Hungary. The Czechs were not advocating or planning the overthrow of single-party rule by the communists, nor were they threatening to withdraw from the Warsaw Pact. They thought that they were simply pursuing a "different road to socialism," a course that was supposed to be acceptable within the socialist community and compatible with the requirements of proletarian internationalism. That they misunderstood the political implications of what they were attempting became evident on August 21, 1968, when

Czechoslovakia was invaded by Soviet forces and small contingents of troops from the four other cosigners of the *Warsaw Letter*.

Subsequently to the intervention, which was clearly in violation of international law and even the principles of socialist international law, Soviet ideologists began to spin out a theory of "limited sovereignty" and "limited self-determination" that applied to all members of the "socialist commonwealth." Thus, in a major article, the CPSU ideologist S. Kovalev, argued:

> Just as, in V. I. Lenin's words, someone living in a society cannot be free of that society, so a socialist state that is in a system of other states constituting a socialist commonwealth cannot be free of the common interests of the commonwealth. The sovereignty of individual socialist countries cannot be counterposed to the interests of world socialism and the world revolutionary movement . . .
>
> The weakening of any link in the world socialist system has a direct effect on all the socialist countries, which cannot be indifferent to this. Thus, the antisocialist forces in Czechoslovakia were in essence using talk about the right to self-determination to cover up demands for so-called neutrality and the C.S.R.'s withdrawal from the socialist commonwealth. But implementation of such "self-determination," that is, Czechoslovakia's separation from the socialist commonwealth, would run counter to Czechoslovakia's fundamental interests and would harm the other socialist countries. Such "self-determination," as a result of which NATO troops might approach Soviet borders and the commonwealth of European socialist countries would be dismembered, in fact infringes on the vital interests of these countries' peoples, and fundamentally contradicts the right of these peoples to socialist self-determination.[16]

Anticipating objections that the application of this new Soviet doctrine violated existing norms of international law, Kovalev argued that every system of law, including international law, is subordinate to the higher law of the class struggle. Accordingly, the national interests of the individual members of the socialist commonwealth must yield to the needs of the collective interest. Needless to say, the Soviet Union, as the leader of the socialist commonwealth, is the arbiter of the common interest. Kovalev thus argues:

> However, in the Marxist conception, the norms of law, including the norms governing relations among socialist countries, cannot be interpreted in a narrowly formal way, outside the general context of the class struggle in the present-day world. . . . Those who speak of the "illegality" of the allied socialist coun-

tries' actions in Czechoslovakia forget that in a class society there is and can be no such thing as nonclass law. Law and the norms of law are subordinated to the laws of the class struggle and the laws of social development.

On November 12, 1968, Leonid Brezhnev authoritatively restated these arguments in what has since been known in the West as the Brezhnev Doctrine.

The CPSU has always advocated that each socialist country determine the concrete forms of its development along the path of socialism by taking into account the specific nature of its national conditions. But it is well known, comrades, that there are common natural laws of socialist construction, deviation from which could lead to deviation from socialism as such. And when external and internal forces hostile to socialism try to turn the development of a given socialist country in the direction of restoration of the capitalist system, when a threat arises to the cause of socialism in that country—a threat to the security of the socialist commonwealth as a whole—this is no longer merely a problem for that country's people but a common problem, the concern of all socialist countries.[17]

The promulgation of the Brezhnev Doctrine reflected a return to the idea of proletarian internationalism in the sense that it was interpreted by Stalin. The notion of "different roads to socialism," which had caused so much grief in both Hungary and Czechoslovakia because it had been understood as a communist euphemism for national self-determination within the socialist universe, was put on the shelf once again. Proletarian internationalism was redefined by the CPSU ideologist Sovetov in November, 1968 as "solidarity with the Soviet state and support of it in the international arena."[18] This redefined proletarian internationalism was to be the cement that would bind the disparate national elements of the Soviet empire together.

The Soviet intervention in Czechoslovakia provoked unprecedented reactions of alarm and concern in those communist countries that were outside or on the fringe of Moscow's total embrace, most notably Romania, Yugoslavia, Albania, and China. This abandonment of the theory of "different roads to socialism" signified a potential threat to their national security. On August 21, the day of the intervention, Nicolai Ceausescu addressed a rally in front of the Romanian Communist party headquarters and stated: "It is inconceivable in the world today, when the peoples are rising to the struggle for defending their national independence, for equality of rights, that a socialist state, that socialist states, should transgress the liberty and independence of another state. There is no justification whatsoever, and no reason can be accepted for admitting for even for a single moment the idea of military intervention in the affairs of a fraternal socialist state."[19]

Of particular concern to Ceausescu was the device the Soviets employed to provide the fig leaf of legitimacy for their intervention—establishing a rival puppet regime and then responding to a call for assistance from that same regime. The Kremlin might feel inclined to apply this technique in any communist country, particularly one like Romania, which had consistently asserted a degree of independence in foreign affairs. Thus, in an address to an extraordinary session of the Romanian parliament convened on August 22, Ceausescu declared:

The troops of the five socialist countries entered Czechoslovakia without having been called by the elected, constitutional, legal bodies of the country, under the pretext of an appeal made by a certain group. However, in the whole international life, it is unanimously known and accepted that relations between parties and states are established exclusively between the legal leaderships of the same and not between groups or persons who do not represent anybody. To admit the abandoning of principles, the introduction of the practice to invoke for one or another action the requests of isolated groups, means to open the road to arbitrariness, to help towards intervention in the affairs of other parties or states, including the military occupation of some countries.[20]

That same day, the Central Committee of the Albanian Communist party issued a statement that declared that "the Warsaw Treaty has ceased to be a pact protecting the socialist countries that are signatories to it. . . . From a peace treaty, the Warsaw Treaty has been turned into a treaty of war for enslavement. From a treaty of defense against imperialist aggression, it has been turned into an aggressive treaty against the socialist countries themselves."[21]

On March 12, 1969, President Tito of Yugoslavia categorically rejected the Brezhnev Doctrine as an unacceptable intrusion on the national sovereignty of socialist states.

In some East European socialist countries the unacceptable doctrine of a "collective," "integrated," and of an essentially limited sovereignty, is appearing. In the name of a supposedly higher level of relationships between socialist countries this doctrine negates the sovereignty of these states and tries to legalize the right of one or more countries according to their own judgement, and if necessary by military intervention to force their will upon other socialist countries. Naturally we reject decisively such a concept as contrary to the basic rights of all nations to independence and contrary to the principles of international law.[22]

On April 1, 1969, in a report to the Ninth Party Congress of the Chinese Communist party, Defense Minister Lin Piao addressed in the most blunt terms the pernicious implications of the doctrine. "In order to justify its aggression and plunder, the Soviet revisionist renegade clique trumpets the so-called theory of 'limited sovereignty,' the theory of 'international dictatorship,' and the theory of 'socialist community.' What does all this stuff mean? It means that your sovereignty is 'limited,' while his is unlimited. You won't obey him? He will exercise 'international dictatorship' over you—dictatorship over the people of other countries, in order to form the 'socialist community' ruled by the new czars, that is, colonies of social imperialism.'"[23]

The Chinese clearly understood what has remained so difficult for many in the West to grasp, namely, the fundamental continuity between czarist and Soviet imperialism. Harrison E. Salisbury observed in the context of Soviet ambitions in Asia:

This recital of Russian imperialist objectives and her setback at the hands of Japan in 1905 may seem ancient history in the contemporary world of Communist ideology and nuclear determent.

Do not be misled.

Soviet Communist propagandists and contemporary historians base themselves upon this history. Today's Soviet goals are rooted in it. You will look in vain for any measurable divergence between the objectives of Russian czarist policy in the Far East and that of today's Soviet leadership. The czarist heroes of the Japanese siege of Port Arthur are today's heroes of Communist Moscow. When Soviet forces entered Port Arthur in 1945 they knelt at the memorial to Port Arthur's defenders of 1905.[24]

The Brezhnev Doctrine clearly represented an attempt to set out a plausible rationale for according legitimacy to Soviet imperialism. What was uncertain at the time of its promulgation was whether it applied outside the Warsaw Pact or outside Eastern Europe. It was to take another decade before the answer to this question became apparent as a consequence of the Soviet intervention in Afghanistan. In April 1978 a Marxist regime came to power through a successful coup. In December, Moscow and Kabul signed a treaty of friendship, good neighborliness, and cooperation. The Marxist takeover, however, was unacceptable to many Afghans who were prepared to register their disapproval through direct action. An insurgency against the Marxist regime broke out and soon spread throughout the country, threatening the regime's continued survival. The Soviet Union, true to its proposition that no state, once acknowledged as a member of the socialist community, may be permitted to reverse its revolutionary course, intervened to prop up the Marxist government in Kabul. Additional problems encountered by the Soviets in the process precipitated an armed intervention in force in December 1979. As Brezhnev put it, "the revolutionary process in Afghanistan [was] irreversible."[25]

At the time of this writing, it seems quite clear that "the Brezhnev Doctrine is very much a part of Gorbachev's policy."[26] Gorbachev has left little doubt that, notwithstanding the current Soviet rhetoric of liberalization, it would be unwise for any members of the socialist community to think in terms of the freedom to opt out of the Soviet orbit. He warned at a congress of the Polish Communist party in June 1986: "Socialism now manifests itself as an international reality, as an alliance of states closely linked by political, economic, cultural and defense interests. To threaten the socialist system, to try to undermine it from the outside and wrench a country away from the socialist community means to encroach not only on the will of the people, but also on the entire postwar arrangement, and, in the final analysis, on peace."[27]

The geopolitical implications of this position with regard to Europe are unequivocal. Eastern Europe belongs to the Soviet empire. In Gorbachev's view this arrangement was conceded by the United States and Great Britain at the Tehran and Yalta conferences during World War II, and any state that attempts to interfere with the status quo in Eastern Europe is endangering world peace. In Asia the status of the peripheral holdings of the empire is less clear, if only because it has not as yet been confirmed by the international community. Soviet hegemony in Mongolia, which has been a vassal of the Soviet Union for more than 50 years, remains a matter of contention between Moscow and Beijing. Chinese interests are intimately affected by its availability as a forward base for Soviet power projection into the heart of China. Vietnam, which appears to be well within Moscow's embrace, is nonetheless separated from the Soviet Union by China, a fact that creates certain very real geostrategic problems for the Kremlin. North Korea, traditionally able to play off the Soviet Union and China against each other, appears to be on the verge of sliding into Soviet satellite status. With regard to Afghanistan, the Soviets are at present seeking to gain recognition of their dominance through negotiations under the auspices of the United Nations. A so-called negotiated settlement of the Afghanistan problem, to be followed by the withdrawal of Soviet forces, will be achieved when Moscow feels confident that its protégé regime in Kabul is capable of maintaining control of the country on its behalf. However, Afghanistan will remain a constituent component of the Soviet empire in Asia and a springboard for its further expansion to the south.

The central thesis of this book is that the next phase of Soviet imperialist expansion will most likely be to the south in the direction of the Indian Ocean. This region is intimately related to the overall security posture of the Soviet empire, and it has particular relevance to the geostrategic problems confronting Moscow as it pursues its ambitions in the Far East and the Pacific Basin. The key to the solution of some of the more pressing of these problems lies in Southwest Asia.

To place this argument in an appropriate historical context, one that will help to explain the concerns of the Soviet government with regard to the geostrategic aspects of its security posture in Asia, chapters 2–5 will consider the pattern and process of expansion over the past several centuries that have brought Russia and the Soviet Union to the contemporary configuration of empire that stretches across much of the land mass of Eurasia. Chapters 6–8 will describe briefly the circumstances through which this phenomenal growth took place, the means by which it was accomplished, the strategic aims it sought to satisfy, and the geostrategic dilemmas that must be dealt with in the not too distant future if the Soviet empire is to remain viable.

Notes

1. George F. Kennan, "The Sources of Soviet Conduct," *Foreign Affairs*, July 1947, p. 572.

2. James T. Westwood, "The Relentless March," *Army*, June 1981, pp. 65–66.

3. Cited by Alexis Krausse, *Russia in Asia: A Record and a Study, 1558–1899*, p. 229.

4. Hans J. Morgenthau, *Politics among Nations*, p. 21.

5. Ibid., p. 27.

6. Cited by William G. Bray, *Russian Frontiers: From Muscovy to Khrushchev*, p. 41.

7. Michael Voslensky, *Nomenklatura*, p. 324.

8. Ibid., p. 320.

9. Boris Meissner, *The Brezhnev Doctrine*, p. 14.

10. *Pravda*, October 31, 1956.

11. Ferenc A. Vali, *Rift and Revolt in Hungary*, pp. 354–55.

12. *Pravda*, December 2, 1959.

13. Milovan Djilas, "The Storm in Eastern Europe," *New Leader*, November 19, 1956.

14. *Pravda*, July 4, 1968.

15. Ibid., July 18, 1968.

16. S. Kovalev, "Sovereignty and the Internationalist Obligations of the Socialist Countries," *Pravda*, September 26, 1968.

17. *Pravda*, November 13, 1968.

18. Cited by Meissner, op. cit., p. 26.

19. Agerpress, *Documents, Articles and Information on Romania*, supplement no. 18, August 21, 1968.

20. Cited by Meissner, op. cit., pp. 75–76.

21. *Peking Review*, April 30, 1969.

22. Cited by Meissner, op. cit., pp. 71–72.

23. *Peking Review*, April 30, 1969.

24. Harrison E. Salisbury, *War between Russia and China*, pp. 9–10.

25. *Washington Post*, October 17, 1980.

26. Dimitri K. Simes, "Gorbachev: A New Foreign Policy?" *Foreign Affairs*, vol. 65, no. 3, 1987.

27. *Pravda*, July 1, 1976.

2   *Expansion in Europe*

The emergence of modern Russia began in the wake of the power vacuum created by the slow disintegration of the Mongol empire of Genghis Khan in the fourteenth and fifteenth centuries. As the Golden Horde broke up into numerous Tartar khanates, the power of the Russian grand duke of Moscow began to increase dramatically, and Moscow became a powerful military state in the mid fifteenth century under the able leadership of Ivan III. By 1480 the duchy of Moscow had rid itself of the last vestiges of vassalage to the Golden Horde and began the reconquest of the traditionally Russian lands contiguous to it. It waged a long and particularly bitter struggle to retrieve the territories in the west that had come under the control of the rulers of Lithuania. Moscow claimed these lands on the basis of a heritage that reached back long before the Mongol conquest. The threat of defeat by Moscow precipitated the union of Lithuania and Poland in 1569, subsequently bringing temporary reversals to Moscow's expansion in Europe.

In the second half of the sixteenth century, Ivan the Terrible expanded the scope of Russian imperial ambitions with an attack against the small Baltic states that blocked Moscow's access to the Baltic Sea and communications with Western Europe. This move brought Moscow into collision with Sweden as well. In 1583, Ivan was forced to conclude a costly peace with both Poland and Sweden. Virtually everything Moscow had retrieved from Lithuania had to be turned over to Poland, and its conquests along the Baltic coast had to be yielded to Sweden. Furthermore, during the troubled years between the death of Fedor, the last czar of the Rurik dynasty, in 1598 and the coronation of the first Romanov czar, Mikhail, in 1613, Poland and Sweden had seized substantial chunks of Russia's western territories. In 1611, after a long siege, Smolensk was taken by the Poles, while Novgorod came under Swedish control. By 1612 the Poles occupied a large slice of Russia bounded by the Dnieper River to the west, the Volga River to the north, and Moscow to the east. By the following year the Swedes controlled northwest Russia from Lake Ladoga south to Lake Ilmen and west to the Gulf of Finland.

The subsequent rallying of the Russians to the new Romanov czar signaled the reassertion of Muscovite power and the reversal of Moscow's fortunes. It also marked the beginning of the new and relentless Russian expansionism that was not limited to recovering mastery over the vast lands that had at one time or another been under Russian control. The initial results of the ensuing struggles with Sweden and Poland were positive but inconclusive. The Peace of Stolbovo (1617) required the Swedes to withdraw from Novgorod. However, they still retained Ingria and the region around Lake Ladoga. Since Sweden had earlier acquired Estonia, this gave it control of the entire littoral of the Gulf of Finland and cut Russia off from access to the Baltic Sea. The Poles, who attempted to attack Moscow in 1618, were forced to withdraw. However, under the terms of the Armistice of Deulino (1618), Poland retained the Russian provinces of Smolensk and Seversk, as well as some additional land along the length of Russia's western border.

The Russians attempted to retake Smolensk in 1632, but to no avail. The subsequent Peace of Polyanovka in 1634 brought about only minor adjustments in the Russo-Polish border. By 1648 long-festering unrest in the Polish-occupied Ukraine finally broke out into open warfare between the Poles and the Zaporozhie Cossacks under the leadership of Bogdan Khmelnitsky. Czar Alexis (1645–76) used the occasion to extend his protection to the Cossacks, which led to a new and protracted war (1654–67) with Poland. This conflict led to the devastation of both the Ukraine and Poland. This time, under the Armistice of Andrusovo (1667), Poland was forced to make significant concessions to Moscow.

Russia gained control of Smolensk, Chernigov, all of the Ukraine east of the Dnieper River, and Kiev on the opposite bank. Under the terms of the armistice, Russian control of Kiev was to be limited to a two-year period. Nonetheless, once having gotten control of the ancient Russian city, Czar Alexis refused to return it to Poland. In 1678 an agreement was finally reached with Poland that confirmed Russia's possession of Kiev in exchange for border rectifications along the northern frontier. In the 1667 armistice agreement, Russia and Poland had also agreed to a joint protectorate over the Sech, the centrol domicile of the Zaporozhie Cossacks. However, in the "Eternal Peace" negotiated between the two countries in 1686, the Poles, no longer able to bargain from a position of strength, were required to turn the region over completely to the Russians.

Notwithstanding its successes at the expense of Poland, Russia was still essentially landlocked and cut off from direct communications with the West. A circuitous and difficult passage from the White Sea had already been opened but was only usable for half the year. Sweden's occupation of the Baltic coast became the next target of Russia. Peter the Great (1682–1725) formed an alliance with Denmark and Saxony, which had their own scores to settle with Sweden, in 1699. However, Peter would not go to war against Sweden until he was certain that he would not be attacked in the south by Turkey. Two-front wars had proven disastrous for Russia in the past, and Peter had no intention of running such a risk now. The onset of the war was thus delayed while peace was being laboriously negotiated with Constantinople. B. H. Sumner has noted: "These negotiations were conducted personally by Peter in the utmost secrecy under the very noses of a special Swedish embassy to Moscow. He succeeded in fobbing off the Swedes with protestations of friendship and the solemn reconfirmation of the previous Russo-Swedish treaties, though his duplicity stopped short of renewing his oath to abide by them."[1]

The alliance that Peter was instrumental in concocting did not turn out as had been expected. While Peter stalled, waiting for the negotiations with Turkey to be completed, Augustus of Saxony launched the Great Northern War alone in January 1700. Denmark joined a few months later. Russia's treaty with Turkey was not signed until July 14, and Peter did not learn of it until August 19. That same day, Russia declared war on Sweden. However, unknown to Peter, that same day,

Denmark signed the Treaty of Travendal, marking the end of its part in the war. This and other factors in combination transformed what was expected to be a relatively short campaign into a twenty-one-year war.

The consequences of the Great Northern War with Sweden (1700–21) were far-reaching. In 1703, Russia conquered Ingria, once again giving Moscow an opening on the Baltic that it was intent on retaining. Saint Petersburg, which Peter made the capital of Russia a decade later, was founded that same year. The Treaty of Nystadt (1721) confirmed Russia's annexation of Ingria, Estonia, Livonia (most of which had never been Russian), and the Dago and Osel islands. Russia also received large tracts of territory in southeastern Finland that included the provinces of Kexholm and Vyborg. Sweden went to war with Russia again 20 years later in an effort to recapture its losses of 1721. The attempt proved counterproductive. By the Treaty of Abo (Turku) of 1743, Sweden was required to cede some additional territory near Vyborg to Russia. The Swedish-Russian frontier along the Gulf of Finland was now set at the Kymi River.

After the death of Peter in 1725, Russian policy in Europe was relatively quiescent for some 40 years, until the accession to power of the Empress Catherine. "If successful aggression be the mark of greatness, Catherine II (1762–96) earned her sobriquet, 'the Great.' ''[2] Her major additions to the Russian empire in Europe were, once again, primarily at Poland's expense. From the first partition of a prostrate Poland in 1772, carried out in conjunction with Prussia and Austria, Russia received and annexed the areas of Polotsk, Vitebsk, Mogilev, and part of Lithuania. This gave Saint Petersburg all of the right bank of the western Dvina River and the entire east bank of the Dnieper. The second partition of Poland in 1793, carried out jointly with Prussia, added to Russia the western Russian territories of Minsk, Podolia, and the eastern part of Volhynia, the Ukraine west of the Dnieper. The third partition, done with the participation of Prussia and Austria in 1795, brought Kurland, the western portion of Volhynia, and the remainder of Lithuania, territories peopled by Ukrainians, Lithuanians, and Letts, into the Russian empire. The frontier followed the Niemen, western Bug, and Dniester rivers. For the first time in its history, Russia now had common borders with Austria and Prussia.

For a very brief period during the Napoleonic Wars, between 1798 and 1807, Russia became a Mediterranean power. Allied with its traditional enemy, the Ottoman Empire, from 1798 to 1805, Russia sailed into the Mediterranean to confront France. During the winter of 1798–99, a Russo-Turkish fleet under the command of Admiral Ushakov drove the French out of the Ionian Islands, which France had taken from Venice the previous year. In 1800 the islands of Corfu, Paxo, Leucas, Ithaca, Zante, Cephalonia, and Cythera were formed into the "Septinsular Republic," formally under Turkish suzerainty but actually under the military control of Russia. In 1806 a Russian force from Corfu occupied Kotor (Cattaro) on the coast of Dalmatia. By the Peace of Tilsit in 1807, Russia was compelled to transfer all these territories to France. It was not in a position to oppose the overwhelming naval power of Great Britain, which insisted on Russian withdrawal from the Mediterranean. Without adequate countervailing maritime capability at their disposal, Russian forces in the Mediterranean could easily be cut off from their home bases. The experience served as an object lesson. The Russians learned the cost of imperial adventures without the ability to control their own lines of communications.

In 1808, seeking control of the entire eastern littoral of the Baltic, Russia invaded Swedish Finland. The following year, it annexed the entire grand duchy of Finland along with the Aaland Islands. This entire large area remained part of the Russian empire until 1917. In 1812, shortly before and in anticipation of Napoleon's invasion of Russia, Alexander I (1801–25) made an unprecedented gesture to the Finns. He returned the western part of the Karelian Isthmus, including Vyborg, as well as the area north of Lake Ladoga, to the grand duchy, which, of course, continued to be part of the Russian empire. The gesture to the Finns was also aimed at buying some good will among the Swedes, in the hope that the latter would not see Napoleon's campaign against Russia as an opportunity to settle their own long-standing account. It was clearly in Russia's interest to do whatever it could to reduce the possibility of having to fight a two-front war.[3]

In the meanwhile, the unnatural alliance between Constantinople and Saint Petersburg, concluded in face of the French threat to the eastern Mediterranean in 1798, had come to an end in 1805. The following year another long war (1806–12) commenced between the two rival empires. The Treaty of Bucharest (1812), which terminated the conflict, added the province of Bessarabia, lying between the Dniester and Pruth Rivers, to the Russian empire.

In 1815 the Vienna settlement that marked the end of the Napoleonic era yielded to Russia most of the former grand duchy of Warsaw, created by Napoleon in 1807 out of parts of Austrian and Prussian Poland. Russia was now in control of the central Vistula basin and the city of Warsaw. Russia had emerged from the Napoleonic Wars as the predominant continental military power, with frontiers that extended deep into Central Europe and Scandinavia. It has been estimated that in the century of expansion in Europe between 1710 and 1815, approximately one million square kilometers were added to the Russian empire.[4]

While peace generally prevailed for a century along Russia's western and northwestern frontiers, confrontation with Turkey continued in spasms of war. In 1829 the Peace of Adrianople awarded to Russia the Danube River delta in addition to some acquisitions in the Caucasus and the eastern Black Sea regions. However, Russia's subsequent defeat in the Crimean War (1854–55) forced it to return the Danube delta region to Turkey. It was also forced to transfer the three southern districts of Bessarabia to the principality of Moldavia, which united with Wallachia in 1859 to become the new independent state of Romania. Southern Bessarabia was subsequently returned to Russia by the Treaty of San Stefano and confirmed by the Treaty of Berlin in 1878. As compensation, Romania received the Danube delta region and most of the Dobrudzha (the region south of the lower Danube). Russia's southwestern boundary remained on the northern bank of the Kiliya mouth of the Danube until World War I. The net result of all these changes was that Russia's European frontiers of 1914 were almost identical with those of 1815.

The Russian Revolution that toppled the czarist regime in 1917 had a dramatic impact on the Russian empire, which started to disintegrate almost at once. The overthrow of the czar served as a cathartic that unleashed long-suppressed but always latent nationalist stirrings. Movements calling for independence appeared everywhere. Neither the provisional government that replaced the czarist regime in March 1917 nor the Bolsheviks, who took power in November, were in a position to prevent these moves toward independence. Beset by internal chaos, and still engaged in the war with Germany, there was little choice but to accept the dissolution of the Russian empire, at least for the time being. Within a year, most of the western territories annexed by Peter I, Catherine II, and Alexander I were detached from Russia.

The problems of the new Soviet government were greatly compounded by the terms of the Treaty of Brest-Litovsk (March 3, 1918), which terminated Russia's participation in World War I. It is summarized by George Vernadsky. "The peace conditions were disastrous for Russia. Eastern Poland, Ukraine, Lithuania, Esthonia, and Latvia were separated from Russia and taken over by Germany. . . . Russia's losses were enormous—26 per cent of her total population; 27 per cent of her arable land; 32 per cent of her average crops; 26 per cent of her railway system; 33 per cent of her manufacturing industries; 73 per cent of her iron industries; 75 per cent of her coal fields."[5]

What the Soviets gained from the peace treaty, however, was more significant in the long run. It gave them the respite necessary to consolidate their political position and to prepare to reconquer those lands that had defected from the empire.

The Ukraine posed an especially difficult problem for the Soviets. In early June, 1917 the Ukrainian Central Council, or Rada, informed the provisional government of its demands for autonomy, including the separation of the twelve provinces with a predominantly Ukrainian population into a special administrative region. As the provisional government stalled and haggled, the Ukrainians began to shift from demands for autonomy to demands for independence. Oddly enough, Lenin advocated that the Bolsheviks support Ukrainian nationalist tendencies as a tactical means of weakening the provisional government. Nonetheless, the true importance of the Ukraine to Russia was reflected in a blunt statement by Piatakov, the head of the Bolsheviks in the Ukraine: "On the whole we must not support the Ukrainians, because their movement is not convenient for the proletariat. Russia cannot exist without the Ukrainian sugar industry, and the same can be said in regard to coal (Donbass), cereals (the black-earth belt), etc. . . . We have before us two tasks: to protect against the measures of the government . . . on the one hand, and to fight against the chauvinistic strivings of the Ukrainians on the other."[6]

Notwithstanding the reversal of the Bolsheviks' temporary alliance with the Rada, once they took power in November 1917, they were unable to derail the Ukrainian independence movement. In January 1918, the Ukrainians declared their independence from Russia and established the Ukrainian People's Republic. It was short-lived in a practical sense because Soviet forces marched on the Ukraine and occupied Kiev on February 8. Matters were complicated, however, by the fact that on the following day, representatives of the Ukrainian People's Republic signed a peace treaty with the Central Powers at Brest-Litovsk. The preamble to the document stated, "Whereas the Ukrainian People has, in the course of the present world war, declared its independence, and has expressed the desire to establish a state of peace between the Ukrainian People's Republic and the Power at present at war with Russia, the Governments of Germany, Austria-Hungary, Bulgaria, and Turkey have resolved to conclude a Treaty of Peace with the Government of the Ukrainian People's Republic."[7]

When the Soviets themselves appeared at Brest-Litovsk the following month to sign their own peace treaty, they were forced to acknowledge the independence of the Ukraine. Article 6 of the Treaty of Brest-Litovsk states: "Russia obligates herself to conclude peace at once with the Ukrainian People's Republic and to recognize the treaty of peace between that State and the Powers of the Quadruple Alliance. The Ukrainian territory will, without delay, be cleared of Russian troops and the Russian Red Guard. Russia is to put an end to all agitation or propaganda against the Government or the public institutions of the Ukrainian People's Republic."[8]

With the collapse of Germany in November 1918, chaos broke loose in the Ukraine. Soviet-backed elements engaged in a power struggle and civil war that lasted until early 1920, when the Soviet Union, backed by its troops, reasserted firm control over the country.

The one permanent loss to the Soviet empire, at least in the sense of the absence of direct Soviet domination, was Finland. Finland proclaimed its independence in December 1917 and was recognized by the Soviet government on January 4, 1918, although the Russian forces there remained in place. The Treaty of Brest-Litovsk reaffirmed the independence of Finland and required the withdrawal of Russian troops from Finland and both troops and fortifications from the Aaland Islands. After the ensuing civil war in Finland and the sporadic fighting in Eastern Karelia had ended, the Russian Soviet Federative Socialist Republic (RSFSR) and the Finnish Republic concluded the Peace Treaty of Dorpat on October 14, 1920. The boundaries between the two countries remained essentially the same as existed between Russia and the grand duchy in 1833, with a few minor revisions in favor of Finland in the far north, which gave it an outlet on the Barents Sea. The treaty also contained a provision supporting in principle the neutralization of the Baltic, the Gulf of Finland, and Lake Ladoga. Relations between Moscow and Helsinki remained proper, and on January 21, 1932 the two countries entered into a nonaggression pact.

With the German invasion of Poland in September 1939, which triggered World War II, the Soviets became particularly concerned about the security of their northern European frontier. The Finnish border was only some 20 miles from Leningrad. Only a few miles beyond the frontier, the Finns had constructed the Mannerheim Line, a string of formidable fortifications that stretched completely across the Karelian Isthmus between Lake Ladoga and the Gulf of Finland. Anchored at both ends by water, the line was fortified in depth and had massive gun emplacements facing Leningrad. The possibility that the Mannerheim Line might fall into German hands in connection with an assault on northern Russia, notwithstanding the Soviet-German nonaggression pact of August 1939, impelled the Soviets to seek to improve their strategic posture in this sensitive region.[9]

In October 1939, Moscow demanded that Finland cede the Karelian Isthmus to the Soviet Union in exchange for a chunk of territory north of Lake Ladoga, and lease it the naval bases located at Hankoe Cape for a period of 30 years. The Finns refused and prepared for the war with the Soviets that broke out on November 26, 1939. In December, the Soviets declared cynically: "The Red Army is going to Finland to aid the Finnish people. Only the Soviet Union, which rejects in principle the forcible seizure of territory and the enslavement of peoples, could consent to lend its military might, not for aggression against Finland and for the enslavement of her people, but to secure Finnish independence, to increase the territory of Finland at the expense of the Soviet Union—to establish friendly relations with Finland."[10]

After a brief but valiant struggle, Finland was compelled to sue for peace. The peace agreement of March 1940 cost Finland about 13 percent of its territory. In addition to the Karelian Isthmus and the lease on Hankoe Cape, which were part of the original Soviet demands, the Finns also lost the city and district of Vyborg, the western and north-western shores of Lake Ladoga, the Finnish parts of the Rybachi and Sredni peninsulas and other land in the Arctic region, and a number of small but strategically important islands in the Gulf of Finland, all of which were annexed by the Soviet Union.[11] In 1944, as the tide of the war turned against Germany, the Soviet Union exploited the opportunity to begin the expansion of its borders in the wake of the German retreat from eastern Europe. The Red Army promptly occupied and annexed the Pechenga region of northern Finland, cutting off the latter's outlet to the Barents Sea and Arctic Ocean, thereby bringing the Soviet Union's northern frontier to the Norwegian border. The annexation was subsequently given legal sanction in the Russo-Finnish peace treaty of 1947. The lease on Hankoe Cape was exchanged for a 50-year lease on a naval base in the Porkkala region, about 12 miles from Helsinki. Finland, however, was permitted to retain its independence.

Latvia's demand for independence was also granted by the Russian democratic provisional government in 1917. In accordance with the Treaty of Berlin (August 27, 1918), which was supplementary to the Treaty of Brest-Litovsk, "Russia, taking account of the condition as present existing in Estonia and Livonia [Latvia], renounces sovereignty over these regions, as well as all interference in their internal affairs."[12] However, with the surrender of Germany and the Central Powers in November 1918, the Soviets promptly reneged on this commitment and invaded Latvia on December 5. The invading force was soon driven out, and relations between the two countries were reestablished by the Treaty of Moscow, August 11, 1920, which again recognized the independence of Latvia. These relations were governed by the Peace Treaty of Riga, March 18, 1921. On February 5, 1932, Latvia and Russia signed a nonaggression pact, which was extended on April 4, 1934 until December 31, 1945. This treaty committed each of the signatories to "refrain from any act of aggression directed against the other and also from any acts of violence directed against the territorial integrity and inviolability of the political independence of the other."[13]

Notwithstanding this commitment, on October 5, 1939, Moscow pressured Latvia into signing a mutual assistance pact that gave the Soviet Union control of the Gulf of Riga and military bases and airfields and provided for the stationing of some 30,000 Soviet troops in the country. In July 1940 the Soviet-installed puppet government proclaimed itself the Latvian Soviet republic and requested Moscow to permit it to join the Soviet Union.

Estonia declared its independence in February 1918 and established a constituent assembly in April 1919. On February 2, 1920, by the Treaty of Tartu, the Soviet Union affirmed its recognition of the independence of Estonia and once again (as it had previously done in the Treaty of Berlin in 1918) renounced "voluntarily and forever all rights of sovereignty formerly held by Russia over the Estonian people and territory."[14] On May 4, 1932, Estonia and the Soviet Union also signed a mutual nonaggression pact. On September 15, 1939, however, with massive forces poised to invade the country, Moscow demanded that Estonia enter into a mutual assistance treaty. The pact, which was signed on September 28, 1939, authorized the stationing of 35,000 troops and provided for an air and naval base in the country. Molotov is reported to have assured the Estonian foreign minister, "We want to confirm that the Government of the Soviet Union has no desire to force upon Estonia, Communism or Soviet regime, nor in general to infringe in the slightest degree the sovereignty of Estonia and the independence of Estonia."[15] Following a well-established Soviet practice, a puppet parliament was put into operation on July 21, 1940, and Estonia was admitted into the Soviet Union on August 6.

As in the cases of Estonia and Latvia, Lithuanian independence was recognized immediately after the Russian Revolution and ignored a year later when, on January 5, 1919, Soviet troops attacked the country. The Soviet forces were repulsed, and, on July 12, 1920, by the Treaty of Moscow, the Soviet government recognized "the sovereignty and independence of the State of Lithuania . . . and voluntarily and forever renounced all sovereign rights possessed by Russia over the Lithuanian people and territory."[16] On December 22, 1926 a nonaggression pact was signed by the two countries. On May 6, 1931, when the pact was extended, the Soviet foreign minister, Maxim Litvinov, stated that the agreement was but "an expression of our constant, termless policy of peace, of which the fundamental element is preservation of independence of the young states which you are representing here."[17] On September 26, 1939, Moscow demanded a mutual assistance pact that would allow 50,000 Soviet troops to be based in Lithuania. The Lithuanians objected vehemently, but to no avail. Stalin insisted: "We consider the creation of military bases on Lithuanian territory as a symbolic gesture . . . whereas we respect the independence of the Lithuanian state. We are disposed to defend its territorial integrity."[18] With Soviet forces concentrated on the Lithuanian border, the desired pact was dutifully signed on October 10, 1939. As with its sister Baltic states, Lithuania was incorporated within the Soviet Union during the summer of 1940.

The disintegration of the Russian empire in the wake of the February revolution presented a unique opportunity to Poland. Thrice partitioned in the eighteenth century, Poland was now situated between the collapsing Russian empire to the east and the defeated German and Austro-Hungarian empires to the west and south. This presented an exceptional opportunity for Poland's reconstitution as a sovereign state. The victorious allies were supportive of this idea because, among other reasons, a strong independent Poland would serve to confine the Soviets well to the east of Western Europe. Once again for tactical reasons, the Bolsheviks came out explicitly in favor of Polish self-determination. On August 29, 1918, only two days after signing the supplemental agreement to the Treaty of Brest-Litovsk, the Soviet Council of People's Commissars issued a decree that stated, in part: "All agreements and acts concluded by the Government of the former Russian Empire with the Governments of the Kingdom of Prussia and the Austro-Hungarian Empire which refer to the partitions of Poland, are irrevocably annulled by the present [decree] as contrary to the principle of national self-determination and to the sense of revolutionary legality of the Russian people which recognizes the inalienable right of the Polish people to independence and unity."[19]

On November 7, 1918 the Polish People's Republic was proclaimed. It was not long, however, before it became obvious that the Soviet rhetoric about self-determination was not to be taken seriously where it involved the Soviet Union itself. Self-determination, in Soviet eyes, was a valuable concept as long as the proletariat controlled the government and elected to join with their class compatriots in Russia in a common political arrangement. Poland, which had its own ideas about its political and national future, could not be allowed to impede Soviet revolutionary aims. The stage was set for conflict.

In early February 1919, Polish troops, moving eastward to establish the new government's authority in the Polish borderlands abutting the Soviet Union, clashed with units of the Red Army, which was on the march into Poland. In April, 1920 the Poles, who had formed an alliance with the anti-Bolshevik Ukrainians, attacked the Ukraine and captured Kiev. The Soviets responded in July with a major offensive that brought their forces dangerously close to Warsaw. It was clear that neither side was capable of a decisive victory. Thus, the inclusive war was settled in a compromise by the Peace of Riga (March 18, 1921), which extended Poland's eastern frontier considerably farther than the Curzon Line earlier proposed by the Allies as the boundary with the Soviet Union. Poland now included parts of White Russia and the Ukraine, as well as the area of Vilna, which had been ceded to Lithuania by Russia in 1920.

On August 23, 1939 the Soviet Union entered into a nonaggression pact with Nazi Germany setting the stage for the German invasion of Poland on September 1 and the start of World War II. Attached to the pact was a "Secret Additional Protocol" that placed Finland and the

Baltic states in the Soviet sphere of interest. With regard to Poland, the respective Soviet and German spheres of interest would be separated by a line of demarcation formed by the Narev, Vistula, and San rivers.[20] On September 17 the Soviets attacked an already weakened Poland in the east as the German blitzkrieg rolled toward Warsaw. Encouraged by the absence of any effective resistance to their invasion, the Soviets soon suggested to the Germans that the original idea of dividing Poland into spheres of interest be transformed into an actual partition of the country and the elimination of any residual Polish state. On September 28 a new Nazi-Soviet pact established the Russo-German border essentially along the lines agreed to in August. As compensation for some additional Polish territory assigned to Germany, the Soviet sphere of interest was extended to include most of Lithuania.[21] This fourth partition of Poland effectively restored the *status quo ante* of 1795, with the addition of eastern Galicia.

Louis Fischer has observed that Stalin was intent on obtaining eastern Poland primarily because of its large Ukrainian population. The Ukrainians were the largest national minority in the Soviet Union and, because of their nationalist sentiments, had been subjected to repeated purges in the 1920s and 1930s. The reunification of the Ukrainian people in a common republic within the Soviet Union could do much to increase their loyalty to the Soviet regime. Similar considerations underlay the interest in reabsorbing the Baltic states. "Stalin was motivated by considerations far removed from the proletarian internationalism of Marx and Engels. Through weakness in 1917 and 1918 Russia had lost the Baltic region and Poland. Through diplomacy in 1939 and power in 1940 Stalin retrieved most of what had been lost. He took back the Baltic states in order to claim the support of patriotic Great Russian nationalists; he was restoring the empire. Nationalism thrives on the protein of territory."[22]

The German-Soviet pact of August 23, 1939 also recognized the Soviet interest in Bessarabia, which had been seized by Romania in January, 1918 amid the chaos that accompanied the establishment of the Soviet state in Russia. The Soviet Union had never acknowledged the legitimacy of Romanian claims of sovereignty over the province. In June 1940 a Soviet ultimatum to Romania brought about a cession of Bessarabia and Northern Bukovina, as well as the town of Gertsa (Herta) and some 150 square miles of territory in Moldavia. In August of the same year, the Moldavian Soviet Socialist Republic (SSR) was formed out of a previously autonomous Soviet region and Romanian-speaking Bessarabia. The Ukrainian-speaking sections of Bessarabia and the Gertsa and Northern Bukovina regions were incorporated into the Ukrainian SSR. This created an 839-mile border between Romania and the Soviet Union and placed Soviet forces threateningly close to the rich Romanian oil fields.

The subsequent break between Germany and the Soviet Union, leading to the latter's reversal of alliances, presented Moscow with unprecedented opportunities for expansion as the German army retreated from Eastern Europe in 1944. Pushing its frontiers farther west than ever before, the Soviet Union annexed the northern part of East Prussia, including Koenigsberg (renamed Kaliningrad in 1946). It is interesting that this piece of territory, because of its strategic location on the Baltic Sea, was made part of the distant RSFSR rather than the contiguous Lithuanian SSR. The latter annexed the territory of Memel, between the lower Niemen River and the Baltic coast, from Germany in 1945.

Czechoslovakian Ruthenia (Transcarpathian Ukraine) was ceded to the Soviet Union by the treaty of 29 June 1945 and was incorporated into the Ukrainian SSR as the Transcarpathian Oblast. As a result of this annexation, the Soviet Union has approximately 60 miles of border with Czechoslovakia and about 75 miles of frontier with Hungary.

In a sense, the basis for the new Soviet empire in Europe was laid at the Tehran Conference, November 27-December 3, 1943, between Roosevelt, Churchill, and Stalin. It was there that the decision was reached, for purposes of successfully prosecuting the war, to divide Europe into two major war zones. The United States and Britain would advance from the west and the Soviet Union from the east. British suggestions that another front be opened in southeastern Europe were opposed by both Roosevelt and Stalin, although for rather different reasons. The U.S. chiefs of the armed forces wanted to concentrate their massive military power on a single front, while Stalin clearly wanted a free hand in the east. Once the latter was assured, it was evident, at least to the Communist parties of Eastern Europe, that this division of the continent into effective spheres of interest would have far-reaching postwar political consequences. They began to prepare for the day when Eastern Europe would be liberated from the Germans.[23]

Although an attempt was made afterward at the Yalta Conference of February 4–11, 1945 to assert an Anglo-American interest in Eastern Europe, it was, as a practical matter, too little too late except with regard to Greece. The Soviet presence on the ground throughout Eastern Europe could not be undone. What remained to be done was to define the spheres of interest of the West and the Soviet Union. This was clearly acknowledged by Churchill during his October 1944 visit to Moscow. He describes his meeting with Stalin as follows:

The moment was apt for business, so I said, "Let us settle about our affairs in the Balkans. Your armies are in Rumania and Bulgaria. We have interests, missions and agents there. Don't let us get at cross-purposes in small ways. So far as Britain and Russia are concerned, how would it do for you to have ninety per cent predominance in Rumania, for us to have ninety per cent of the say in Greece, and go fifty-fifty in Yugoslavia?" While this was being translated, I wrote on a half-sheet of paper:

Rumania	Russia 90%
	The others 10%
Greece	Great Britain (in accord with USA) 90%
	Russia 10%
Yugoslavia	50–50%
Hungary	50–50%
Bulgaria	Russia 75%
	The others 25%

I pushed this across to Stalin, who had by then heard the translation. There was a slight pause. Then he took his blue pencil and made a large tick upon it and passed it back to us. It was all settled in no more time than it takes to set it down.[24]

With the exception of Greece, however, it was already too late for the Western allies to influence events in the east significantly. Soviet forces were daily shaping new political realities in Eastern Europe, which was absorbed almost entirely into the Soviet sphere of influence.

Notes

1. B. H. Sumner, *Peter the Great and the Emergence of Russia*, p. 53.
2. Allen F. Chew, *An Atlas of Russian History*, p. 60.
3. Edward C. Thaden, *Russia's Western Borderlands, 1710–1870*, pp. 88–89.
4. Ibid., p. 5.
5. George Vernadsky, *A History of Russia*, p. 265.

6. Cited by Richard Pipes, *The Formation of the Soviet Union*, p. 68.
7. U.S. Department of State, *Texts of the Ukrainian "Peace"*, p. 9.
8. U.S. Department of State, *Texts of the Russian "Peace"*, p. 179.
9. Vernadsky, op. cit., pp. 443–44.
10. *Pravda*, December 4, 1939.
11. Chew, op. cit., p. 100.
12. U.S. Department of State, *Texts of the Russian "Peace"*, p. 179.
13. Cited by William G. Bray, *Russian Frontiers: From Muscovy to Khrushchev*, p. 76.
14. Ibid., p. 77.
15. Ibid.
16. Ibid., p. 78.
17. Ibid., pp. 78–79.
18. Ibid., p. 79.
19. Piotr S. Wandycz, *Soviet-Polish Relations 1917–1921*, p. 61.
20. R. J. Sontag and J. S. Brodie, eds., *Nazi-Soviet Relations, 1939–1941: Documents from the Archives of the German Foreign Office*, p. 78.
21. Ibid., pp. 96–108.
22. Louis Fischer, *Russia's Road from Peace to War*, p. 373.
23. Ghita Ionescu, *The Break-Up of the Soviet Empire in Eastern Europe*, p. 14.
24. Winston Churchill, *Triumph and Tragedy*, p. 227.

3   Expansion to the South

In the late eighteenth century a document appeared in Europe that was alleged to be the last will and testament of Peter the Great. Long known to be spurious, it was apparently intended to blacken the name of Russia for reasons that are not entirely clear. Nevertheless, among other matters, it purported to set forth some of the strategic aims of the Russian empire. Counterfeit or not, it remains a fairly prescient summarization of czarist imperial aims as well as those of the Soviet Union. It enjoined future Russian rulers: "To approach as near as possible to Constantinople and India. Whoever governs there will be the true sovereign of the world. Consequently excite continual wars, not only in Turkey, but in Persia. Establish dockyards on the Black Sea. . . . And in the decadence of Persia, penetrate as far as the Persian Gulf, reestablish if it be possible the ancient commerce with the Levant, advance as far as India, which is the depot of the world."[1]

During the seventeenth century, the czars had indeed attempted repeatedly to break through to the Black Sea coast, which had been under the control of the Ottoman Turks since 1475. From the perspective of Russia's economic development, this was essential. Much of the commerce within Russia took place along its major rivers. One of these, the Don, emptied into the Sea of Azov, which in turn opened into the

Black Sea. Farther west there were the Dnieper, the southern Bug, and the Dniester, all of which emptied into the Black Sea within a relatively short distance of one another. As a consequence, whoever controlled the northern shore of the Black Sea could also control much of the river trade of Russia.[2]

A move to gain control of this strategically important coastal area precipitated a long war against the Ottoman Empire (1676–81), which failed, however, to achieve the Russian goal. Again in 1687, Basil Golitsyn, on behalf of the regent Sophia, tried twice to attack the Crimea directly. These efforts failed primarily because the Russian forces were operating at long distances from their home bases and were plagued by the lack of adequate lines of communication and, most importantly, by the lack of effective control over the critical supply routes. This enabled the Crimean Tartar forces to harass the Russian supply lines, making it impossible for the Russian commanders to sustain the level of effort necessary to conquer the coastal region.[3] Having learned the implicit lesson in this again from his own bitter experience, in 1696 Peter the Great was successful in turning the tables on the Turks. He managed to cut the Turkish lines of communication and captured Azov, giving Russia direct access to the Black Sea. He promptly selected a site at Taganrog for Russia's first naval base. The Russian position on the Black Sea was formally accepted by the Turks in the Treaty of Constantinople (1700).

It was not long, however, before war between the two empires broke out once more. This time Peter found his lines cut once more, his army trapped at the Pruth River and surrounded by a much larger Turkish Tartar force in 1711. The failure to protect his lines of communication cost him dearly. In accordance with the Treaty of Adrianople (1713), the Russian gains in the Azov region had to be abandoned along with Peter's new Black Sea fleet. In addition, the Zaporozhie Cossacks now came under Turkish control. Nonetheless, this was to be the last time that the Ottoman Empire confronted the Russian empire and won.

The drive to the south against the Turks continued under Peter's successors. The war of 1736–39 saw the Russian recapture of Azov and the conquest of both sides of the Don River estuary. The Treaty of Belgrade (1739) also awarded to Russia the region between the southern Bug and the Don rivers north of the narrow strip along the Black Sea coast still controlled by the Crimean Tartars. This included all of Zaporozhie. The region remained unstable for some decades, however. In

1752, two regiments of Serbs were settled on the right bank of the Dnieper River, the eastern boundary of Zaporozhie, to help maintain control over the troublesome Cossacks.

As the result of two successful wars with the Ottoman Empire, Catherine II was able to annex most of the northern shore of the Black Sea. The Treaty of Kuchuk-Kainardji in 1774 gave Russia a foothold on the shore between the southern Bug and Dnieper rivers, including the port of Kherson. Under its terms, for the first time Russian merchant ships were allowed the right of unimpeded navigation in the Black Sea and the right of innocent passage through the Turkish Straits. In addition, the Crimean Peninsula was declared independent of Turkey, and Russia annexed the ports of Kerch and Enikale on its eastern shore. The vaunted independence of the Crimean Tartars lasted only a short time until their state was virtually compelled to accede to formal annexation by Russia in 1783. This gain gave the Russians undisputed control of both sides of the Sea of Azov as far as the Kuban River to the southeast. It also brought to an end the centuries-long struggle of the Russians with the Crimean descendants of the Batu Mongols. In 1792 the Treaty of Jassy not only legitimated the annexation of the Crimea, it also turned over the northwestern coast of the Black Sea between the southern Bug and the Dniester rivers, including the ports of Ochakov and Odessa. Catherine the Great had succeeded in making Russia a Black Sea power and in enlarging the empire by some 200,000 square miles of territory.

Alexander I pursued a consistent policy of further weakening the Turks in every way possible. One method was to encourage separatist and revolutionary movements within the Ottoman Empire. An ostensibly Greek organization called the *Hetairia Philike* (Friends of Antiquity) was founded in Odessa and was led by a Russian army officer, Alexander Ipsilanti.[4] In 1821, Ipsilanti initiated an abortive revolt against the Turks, which helped trigger a more serious outbreak in southern Greece. The Turkish moves to suppress the revolt brought a Russian ultimatum to the Sultan, Mahmud II. However, before a war could break out, both Great Britain and Austria intervened and dissuaded Alexander from carrying out his threat. "What the Austrians and British really feared," according to Warren B. Walsh, "was unilateral Russian action which might have led to Russian gains."[5]

Alexander's policy with regard to the Turks was continued by Nicholas I, who also contemplated a unilateral move to alter the status quo. Once again the British intervened. They talked Nicholas into joining with them in a cooperative venture against the Ottoman Empire. This was worked out in the Petersburg Agreement of 1826. The Turks were urged to grant Greece autonomous status within the Ottoman Empire and thereby avert a joint Anglo-Russian intervention. The sultan, taken aback by this unanticipated alliance against him, quickly proceeded to attempt to split the allies by making a separate deal with Russia that would satisfy some of its long-standing aims in the region.

Under the Convention of Akkerman (1826), the sultan agreed to accept the border changes in the Caucasus that the czar was insisting upon as well as to permit Russian merchant ships to pass unhindered through the Turkish Straits. Finally, though the sultan also agreed to respect the autonomy of Serbia, he remained unwilling to reach a similar accommodation with respect to Greece. Notwithstanding Russian agreement to these terms, the czar also reaffirmed Russia's adherence to the Petersburg Agreement, which, by the Treaty of London (1827), was transformed into a trilateral alliance that now included France.

The British and French purpose in concocting this tripartite arrangement was to place additional constraints on unilateral Russian action against the Porte that might further destabilize Ottoman rule at that particular time. However, things did not work out as expected. An unintended series of tactical missteps brought about the destruction of the Turko-Egyptian fleet on October 20, 1827 by a combined alliance squadron in Navarino Bay. The net result was a significant weakening of Ottoman power, precisely what was not desired by either Great Britain or France. The sultan nonetheless continued to refuse to cooperate with regard to the question of autonomy for the Greeks. It was not long before Nicholas's agreement with Great Britain and France crumbled and, on April 26, 1828, Russia declared war on Turkey once again.

Russia's war aims seemed to be uncertain. After capturing Adrianople in August 1829 and coming threateningly close to Constantinople, instead of pursuing his advantage Nicholas offered peace terms to Mahmud. Though Nicholas announced that he was not interested in capturing Constantinople, it is difficult to reconcile this with the tremendous strategic and economic benefits that would have accrued to the Russian empire through control of the Turkish Straits. "But if he really wanted Constantinople, why didn't he make the most of this very excellent opportunity to take it? The answer seems to lie in the military situation. The Russian army which had crossed the Balkan mountains and captured Adrianople was dangerously exposed at the end of long and uncertain lines of communication."[6]

The Treaty of Adrianople (September 14, 1829), which terminated the conflict, yielded some small but significant gains for Russia. The Russian frontier was moved from the northern mouth of the Danube to the southern. This placed Russia in a position to control the entire Danube delta and enhanced its influence in the lands along the river's long course. In addition, the Ottomans also recognized Russian sovereignty over Georgia and Circassia. Finally, the provinces of Moldavia and Wallachia were made virtually independent under the nominal sovereignty of Turkey, while the idea of Greek autonomy was also now accepted in principle. The intriguing question is why Russia did not pursue its advantage and exploit the opportunity to eliminate the Ottoman Empire in Europe and establish its own dominance over the entire northern littoral of the Black Sea.

Nicholas had appointed a special Committee of Seven in 1829 to consider the several options open to him with regard to the Ottomans. The group recommended against forcing the Turks out of Europe. It believed that such a move at the time would prove counterproductive. Given Russian expansion in the Caucasus and Transcaucasia, it expressed concern that the ejection of the Turks might generate a unification of the Muslim nations on Russia's southern flank under the Ottoman banner to oppose them across Asia as far as China. If the Ottoman Empire were to be partitioned, there was no way that Russia could stop Austria, France, and Great Britain from sharing in the spoils. This would have the undesirable consequence of replacing a weak neighbor to the south with three powerful ones, each of which was itself bent on empire. Furthermore, internationalization of the Turkish Straits, while reducing some of Russia's strategic concerns about freedom of egress from the Black Sea, would at the same time give France and Great Britain, with their far more formidable fleets, freedom of passage too close to Russia's own backyard. This led to the conclusion that prudence required Russia to preserve a weak Turkey that would be at peace with it, at least for the time being, not because of any diminution of Russian imperial ambitions but because the situation called for dilatory tactics. The czar accepted the recommendation of the special committee. Years later, in 1844, Nicholas is reported to have stated, "I do not wish to establish myself in Constantinople, [but] I shall never consent to either England or France establishing herself there."[7]

Nicholas's policy was to nurture the Ottomans only as long as it would serve to keep the other European states out of the region. Were Turkey to collapse of its own accord, it was Russia's task to be prepared to pick up the pieces. Russia thus came to the sultan's aid when he was confronted by a military challenge from Mehmet Ali of Egypt over Syria in 1833. Nicholas extracted a price, which was set out in the Treaty of Unkiar Skelessi (July 1833), for his help. The treaty established an eight-year defensive alliance between the Russian and Ottoman empires and granted Russia the exclusive right of intervention in Turkey. This suggested that the sultan was becoming a de facto vassal of the czar. Also appended was a secret clause that dealt with the closure of the straits, but whose precise terms were never made public. Presumably, it assured that the straits would remain closed to foreign warships, and it was interpreted in this manner in London.

The revolutions of 1848 struck every country in Europe except Britain and Russia. Nicholas sensed the danger to the continued stability of the Russian system and undertook to intervene throughout the lands on or near his frontiers. He promptly suppressed nationalist disturbances in Moldavia and Wallachia. In 1849 the Russian army went into Hungary and quelled the rebellion there on behalf of Austria. In 1850, Nicholas pressured Prussia to subordinate itself once again to Austrian dominion, as had been agreed in 1815. Russia had arrogated to itself the role of the policeman of Europe, a role that was clearly unacceptable to both Britain and France.

In 1853, Nicholas sought to redefine Russian rights in the Holy Places in Palestine and, generally, as the protector of the Christians in the Ottoman Empire. Sensing an emerging anti-Russian coalition of Britain and France, the sultan refused to meet the Russian demands. On July 3, Russia marched into Moldavia and Wallachia, which, though nominally tributary to Turkey, were in fact Russian protectorates. The other great powers proposed a compromise, which was acceptable to Nicholas but was rejected by the sultan. Emboldened by the prospect of support by the two Western European powers, Turkey crossed the Danube on October 27 and attacked Russia. On March 28, 1854, Britain and France also declared war on Russia.

The Crimean War went badly for Russia and, at the end of 1855, the new czar, Alexander II, had little choice but to accept the terms offered by Britain, France, and Austria. The Treaty of Paris (March 30, 1856) reversed many of the gains that Russia had made in Europe since the Napoleonic era. Britain, France, and Austria were to appoint a commission to oversee the freedom of navigation on the Danube, the Russian protectorate over Moldavia and Wallachia was replaced by a

Great Power guarantee, and a portion of Bessarabia was detached and assigned to the Danubian provinces. However, as is suggested by Graham Stephenson, "the most important—and the least wise—portion of these agreements concerned the neutralisation of the Black Sea. This clause was forced through by Britain and Austria. It handicapped Russia far more than Turkey; for whereas it was virtually impossible for any warship to enter the Black Sea it was simple for Turkey (or her British ally) to keep a fleet just south of the Bosporus and to pass it into the Black Sea in case of war against Russia. Thus the results of a century of Russian advance in the Black Sea area were threatened."[8] From 1856 to 1871 the primary concern of Russian policy was to find a means of undoing the Black Sea clauses. The opportunity finally came after a series of events in Europe caused the Crimean alliance to collapse. In October 1870, Russia unilaterally renounced the Black Sea clauses of the Treaty of Paris.

Russian ambitions in the region received significant reinforcement from its experience in the Russo-Japanese War of 1904–5. The Russian fleet had to travel 20,000 miles from the Baltic to the Sea of Japan, along a route around Africa devoid of any bases or ports it could put into for supplies and repairs. By contrast, had the route through the Mediterranean and the Suez Canal been available for a fleet operating from the Black Sea, the trip would have been reduced almost by half. When World War I broke out, and Russia found itself allied with Great Britain and France against Germany and Turkey, it saw this as the long-awaited opportunity to fulfill its aim in the Middle East. In March 1915, Britain and France, in a reversal of long-standing policy resulting from the exigencies of war, accepted Russian claims for the postwar annexation of both shores of the Bosphorus, the Dardanelles, the Sea of Marmara, and Constantinople. Aaron Klieman noted: "With Turkey prostrate by 1917, at last success was within Russia's reach. In view of the current Soviet appreciation for the Mediterranean, it is ironic that at that decisive moment Bolshevik renunciation of all earlier tsarist territorial claims should have kept Russia from at least sharing dual control of this area with Britain," until the present.[9]

Following its War of Independence (1919–22), which was sealed by the Peace Treaty of Lausanne (July 24, 1923), Turkey pursued a foreign policy characterized by the avoidance of alliances and entanglements, coupled with the attempt to build friendly relations with all the major powers, but most especially with its immediate neighbors. In March

1921, Turkey signed a treaty of mutual friendship with the Soviet Union, its first with a major power. This was supplemented in 1925 by a treaty of neutrality and nonaggression.

The Treaty of Lausanne also provided for an international regime over the straits, the International Straits Commission. By 1936, however, the security situation in Europe had changed dramatically for the worse as compared to 1923. The vulnerability of the demilitarized straits was seen by Turkey as a threat to its national security. The guarantees of Turkish security by the signatory powers to the Straits Convention were no longer credible in that, according to the view of the Turkish government, they "have become uncertain and inoperative in that they can no longer in practice shield Turkey from an external danger to her territory."[10] The Soviet Union was very supportive of Turkey's request for an international conference to consider changes to the regime of the straits. The Soviets believed that it would be to their advantage if a new Straits Convention restored Turkish sovereignty over the waterway. This would remove external powers from control over the straits and permit the Soviet Union to reach its own accommodation with Turkey on a matter of such intrinsic importance to it.[11] The Turkish proposal received general support, and the Conference of Montreux (June 22–July 20, 1936) was convened.

The revision of the Treaty of Lausanne proposed by Turkey was highly favorable to the Soviet Union. Whereas the total tonnage that non–Black Sea states might pass through the straits into the Black Sea was drastically curtailed, the only new limits imposed on the egress of the Soviet fleet from the Black Sea concerned the size and type of the units actually passing the straits at any one time and not the total tonnage involved. A British analyst noted at the time:

The Soviet fleet, in other words, would now obtain a preponderant position within the Black Sea without sacrificing its potential influence in the Mediterranean, and in case of war would be able to attack a hostile fleet in the Mediterranean and then retire to the Black Sea without risk of effective pursuit. This together with the fact that Turkey might give permission to any fleet of any size to pass the Straits during a war in which she herself was a belligerent, meant that so long as Turco-Soviet relations continued to be as good as they had been in the past, the position of Soviet Russia would be greatly strengthened.[12]

Britain fought the adoption of the Turkish draft with great determination and succeeded in forcing the adoption of some important compromises that became necessary to assure its concurrence with the new draft agreement. The Montreux Convention of 1936 reversed the demilitarized status of the Bosporus and the Dardanelles, restored control over the straits to Turkey, and set the new rules for their use by ships of foreign flags. From the Soviet perspective, the convention that was finally adopted was still quite favorable to the Soviet Union and greatly strengthened its potential role in the Mediterranean, provided that Turkey remained friendly and neutral.

Turko-Soviet relations took a turn for the worse as war in Europe came closer. After disclosure of the German-Soviet Nonaggression Treaty of August 23, 1939, the Turkish foreign minister was invited to Moscow to discuss a mutual assistance pact. Among the Soviet demands was the insistence that the Montreux Convention be modified to give the Soviet Union joint control over the straits. It has been suggested by Altemur Kiliç that one of the reasons why the Soviets were pressing the question of the straits at this particular time was that Moscow had designs on Bessarabia. Britain and France, however, had guaranteed Romanian independence; thus, if they were to come to Romania's aid, they would have to transit the Turkish Straits to do so, and, in accordance with the Montreux Convention, Turkey would be obliged to permit their fleets to enter the Black Sea.[13] The Soviet demands were deemed unacceptable by Turkey, and the talks were broken off. Within two days after its ambassador left Moscow, Turkey entered into a treaty of mutual assistance with France and Great Britain on October 19, 1939. Turkey nonetheless managed to stay neutral until nearly the end of World War II.

It was clear to the Turks that Soviet ambitions with regard to the regime of the Turkish Straits remained fundamentally the same as those of their czarist predecessors, aims they had ostensibly renounced in 1918. Moscow was again seeking nothing less than effective control of the strategically critical waterway. Indeed, unknown to the Turks at the time, during the 1940 Nazi-Soviet negotiations over postwar spheres of interest, the Soviet Union insisted on the need for freedom of naval movement through the straits as an essential minimum ingredient of any agreement. When Molotov visited Berlin on November 12–13, 1940, Ribbentrop submitted a draft agreement to him that included a secret protocol that stated: "Germany, Italy, and the Soviet Union will work in common toward the replacement of the Montreux Straits Convention now in force by another convention. By this convention the Soviet Union would be granted the right of unrestricted passage of its navy through the Straits at any time, whereas all other Powers except the other Black Sea countries, but including Germany and Italy, would in principle renounce the right of passage through the Straits for their naval vessels. The passage of commercial vessels through the Straits would, of course, have to remain free in principle.''[14]

For the Soviets, this did not go far enough, and they submitted a counterdraft on November 26, which called for, among other things, modification of the protocol delineating Soviet interests in the area of the Straits: ''Likewise, the draft of the protocol or agreement between Germany, Italy, and the Soviet Union with respect to Turkey should be amended so as to guarantee a base for light naval and land forces of the U.S.S.R. on the Bosporus and the Dardanelles by means of a long-term lease.''[15] This aspect of the Molotov-Ribbentrop negotiations was, however, never implemented since the Germans rejected other parts of the Soviet demands relating to Eastern Europe.

The subsequent collapse of the Nazi-Soviet pact and Moscow's reversal of alliances did little to assuage Turkey's concerns. As suggested by Ferenc A. Vali, ''Turkey realized that she would have to confront the Soviets as soon as the hostilities ended. This realization was the main reason for avoiding any involvement in the hostilities with Germany which would weaken her already outdated war potential.''[16]

As the war was coming to an end, Stalin again raised the straits question at the Yalta Conference on February 10, 1945. He maintained that the Montreux Convention had to be revised to give more realistic consideration to Soviet interests. He took the position that ''it was impossible to accept a situation in which Turkey had a hand on Russia's throat.''[17] Though there was general agreement in principle that the Montreux Convention needed revision, no specific decisions in this regard were adopted. At the Potsdam Conference in July, Stalin raised the matter once again, but he was unable to get any agreement from Truman and Churchill on Soviet interests in the straits beyond a general concurrence that the convention needed revision.

On March 19, 1945 the Soviet Union informed Turkey that it did not intend to extend the treaty of neutrality and nonaggression of 1925, which was due to expire in November of the year, unless appropriate changes were made to reflect the new postwar realities. In June, Moscow proposed that Turkey return the provinces of Kars and Ardahan to the Soviet Union and allow it to establish bases on the straits. On December 20 an article by two members of the Academy of the Georgian Soviet Socialist Republic was published simultaneously in *Pravda* and *Izvestia* claiming "historic rights" that went beyond the two Turkish provinces to include a substantial section of the Turkish Black Sea coast.[18] This was seen in Turkey as both threatening and highly provocative since, only about a week earlier, Soviet puppet governments had been established in Iranian Azerbaijan and Kurdistan, areas abutting Turkey's eastern frontiers.

On January 5, 1946, President Truman wrote: "There isn't a doubt in my mind that Russia intends an invasion of Turkey and the seizure of the Black Sea Straits to the Mediterranean. Unless Russia is faced with an iron fist and strong language another war is in the making. Only one language do they understand—'how many divisions have you?' "[19]

The Soviets continued to press without any success their demand for a base in the straits throughout the following year. This had the effect of seriously antagonizing the Turks and completely eliminating the possibility of close relations between the two states for almost 20 years. On August 7, 1946, Moscow initiated the formal procedure for requesting a revision to the Montreux Convention with a note declaring that the existing agreement "does not meet the interests of the safety of the Black Sea Powers." In its note to the signatory states, the Soviet Union proposed two principles that again reflected its desire to gain control of the vital waterway:

The establishment of a regime of the Straits, as the sole sea passage leading from the Black Sea and to the Black Sea, should come under the competence of Turkey and other Black Sea powers.

Turkey and the Soviet Union, as the powers most interested and capable of guaranteeing freedom of commercial navigation and security in the Straits, shall organize joint means of defense of the Straits for the prevention of the utilization of the Straits by other countries for aims hostile to the Black Sea powers.[20]

Predictably, Ankara rejected the notion of a condominium with the Soviet Union over the straits. On August 22 it informed Moscow that, among other things, joint defense of the straits was "not compatible with the inalienable rights of sovereignty of Turkey nor with its security, which brooks no restriction."[21] Again, on October 18, 1946, Ankara noted that the Soviet proposal to close the Black Sea to nonriparian powers "would put the other riverain States at the mercy of the maritime power which possessed the strongest land forces, in other words, at the mercy of the USSR itself."[22] The Soviet Union and Turkey thus remained deadlocked, and Moscow soon dropped its effort to revise the Montreux Convention, primarily because it knew that it could not get the support of the United States and Great Britain for its proposal. The continuing threat posed by Stalin's unabashed ambitions in Turkey led Ankara into the North Atlantic Treaty Organization (NATO) on February 18, 1952.

After the death of Stalin in March 1953, the Soviets took a different approach to Turkey. Moscow formally withdrew its territorial claims on May 30, 1953 and suggested that its outstanding differences with Turkey over the straits were amenable to a mutually agreeable solution. In a declaration that must have drawn cynical smiles in Ankara, the Soviet Union stated:

In the name of preserving good neighborly relations and strengthening peace and security, the Governments of Armenia and Georgia have found it possible to renounce their territorial claims on Turkey.

Concerning the question of the Straits the Soviet Goverment has reconsidered its former opinion on this question and considers possible the provision of security of the U.S.S.R. from the side of the Straits on conditions acceptable alike to the U.S.S.R. and Turkey. Thus the Soviet Government declares that the Soviet Union has not any kind of territorial claims on Turkey.[23]

The Turks, however, still wary of Soviet intentions, remained aloof in the face of this new overture. The Soviet gambit was widely seen as a ploy to placate Turkey as a means of weakening NATO on its southern flank. Relations between Ankara and Moscow were to remain cool for another decade.

Matters took a turn for the better after the Turkish clash with the United States over Turkey's Cyprus policy in 1964. When the Soviets supported Turkey, at least until the Turkish military intervention a decade later, relations moved rapidly toward normalization. Since then, the Soviet Union has apparently been pursuing a carrot-and-stick policy designed to distance Turkey from the NATO alliance and steer it toward neutrality. On the one hand, it has continued to develop closer economic ties between the two countries. On the other hand, through military exercises and other means, it emphasizes the dangers facing Turkey in the event of its possible involvement in a NATO–Warsaw Pact conflict in which Turkey should have only a marginal national interest.

The Soviet Union is also in a position to apply pressure on Turkey indirectly through its satellite, Bulgaria. European Turkey (Turkish Thrace), one of the most densely populated and developed regions of Turkey, lacks both natural barriers and strategic depth. Wedged between Greece and Bulgaria to the north and the Turkish Straits to the south, it is highly vulnerable to attack. Its 269-kilometer border with Warsaw Pact member Bulgaria remains a constant source of security concern to Ankara.[24]

The Caucasus

The Russians had penetrated Kabarda, about midway between the Black and the Caspian seas and just north of the Caucasus Mountains, as far as the Terek River in the sixteenth century, and some Russian troops had been stationed there as a consequence of the marriage of Ivan the Terrible to the daughter of the Kabardian chieftain, Temriuk.[25] However, they were not able to gain a firm grip on the unruly area. Russia had also attempted, again unsuccessfully, to pacify the adjacent region of Daghestan. These early efforts came to an end in 1594 with the defeat of a Russian force led by Prince I. A. Khvorostinin and the loss of some 3,000 men.[26] Russian interest in the Caucasus region was renewed in the eighteenth century as Persia was distracted by internal chaos and Turkish power was in decline. Under the 1774 Treaty of Kuchuk-Kainardji, Russia received the Kabarda region from Turkey. However, the fierce resistance of the indigenous peoples did not permit the region to become effectively incorporated within the Russian empire until about 1825. The adjoining region of Osetia also came under partial Russian control in 1774 and was annexed in 1806.

In the interim the Russians penetrated south of Mozdok, north of the Terek River in Kabarda, and reached Georgia through the Daryal Pass on the upper Terek. In 1784 they established Vladikavkaz, which became the northern terminal of the Georgian military road leading to Tiflis in the heart of the country. A year earlier, the kingdom of Eastern Georgia, comprised of the kingdoms of Kartlia and Kakhetia and facing a threat to its existence from Persia, voluntarily accepted a Russian offer of protection. The Treaty of Georgiyevsk (July 24, 1783) provided for a Russian guarantee of Georgia's independence and territorial integrity in exchange for a Georgian recognition of Russian suzerainty. However, when Agha Mohammed of Persia invaded the country in 1795, leaving Tiflis in ruins, the Russians failed to honor the treaty. Nevertheless, Russian control over the kingdom continued to increase, and on February 16, 1801, Eastern Georgia was incorporated into the Russian empire.

Over the next decade the remaining small states of western Georgia came under the imperial umbrella. The Russian pattern of expansion followed a two-step process that sometimes stretched over a half-century or longer. First the targeted territory was made a protectorate, and then, some years later, it became absorbed through formal annexation. Thus, Mingrelia came under Russian control in 1803 and was annexed in 1857. Imeretia, Guria, and Svanetia all became protectorates about 1804 and were annexed in 1810, 1830, and 1864 respectively. Similarly, Abkhazia received protectorate status in 1810 and joined the empire in 1867.

These inroads into a region that Persia considered to be within its sphere of influence led to war between it and Russia from 1804 to 1813. During this period, Russia seized the Shuragel region and conquered the khanates of Gandzha, Karabakh, Shirvan, Sheki, Baku, Derbent, Kuba, and Talysh, which in the aggregate constituted northern Azerbaijan. Under the Treaty of Gulistan (October 12, 1813), Russia received the exclusive right to maintain a navy in the Caspian Sea, which thus became a Russian lake. Furthermore, Persia was required to accept Russian control of Georgia and to cede both Daghestan and northern Azerbaijan, legitimating the Russian conquests. The southern portion of Daghestan (Dzharo-Belokany and Ilisuyski), however, was not pacified until 1821. It was annexed to Russia in 1830. In the northern part of the region, a native guerrilla leader, Sheykh Shamil, declared a holy war against Russia in 1834. Under Shamil's leadership, northern Daghestan resisted Russian control for another 25 years until he capitulated at Gunib in 1859.

A new war with Persia (1826–28) resulted in the Treaty of Turkmanchai (February 22, 1828), under which Russia received the eastern Armenian khanates of Erevan and Nakhichevan. The approximately 430-mile border between the two countries west of the Caspian Sea has remained, except for minor negotiated border revisions, essentially the same since 1828.

Under the Treaty of Adrianople (1829) the province of Akhaltsikh was transferred by Turkey to Russia, to be rejoined with Georgia. Russia also received the remainder of the northern coast of the Black Sea, including the ports of Anapa, Sukhumi, and Poti. Between 1830 and 1864, Circassia or Cherkesy (between the Black Sea and the Kuban and Laba rivers) was subjugated incrementally. The final Russian acquisitions in Transcaucasia were the provinces of Kars and Ardahan, wrested from the Turks in the Treaty of San Stefano, following the Russo-Turkish War of 1877–78. The Russian empire now included all the lands of Transcaucasia north of a jagged line running between the southern littorals of the Caspian and Black seas.

After the Russian Revolution in March 1917, the Georgians, Armenians, and Azerbaijanis formed the Transcaucasian Federative Republic on September 20. However, it fell apart within a few months. The country then became the independent Georgian Democratic Republic on May 26, 1918. Concerned about the credibility of the Bolsheviks' anti-imperialist protestations, Georgia signed a treaty of friendship with Germany at Poti two days later. On May 28, Armenia and Azerbaijan also declared themselves independent republics. On June 4, Georgia signed a peace treaty with Turkey at Batum, which was under Turkish occupation, that ceded Batum, Artvin, and Ardahan to Turkey. Armenia and Azerbaijan were forced to sign similar treaties, which, in the case of Armenia, required the cession of Kars to Turkey. With the defeat of the Central Powers, German and Turkish forces were withdrawn and replaced by British troops on December 27, 1918. On January 15, 1920 the Allied powers accorded de facto recognition to the three Transcaucasian republics.

It was not long before the new Soviet government turned its attention to the reconquest of Transcaucasia. The decision appears to have been made on March 17, 1920. On that date, Lenin wired Ordzhonikidze instructions to organize the invasion. "It is highly, highly necessary for us to take Baku. Exert all efforts in this direction, but at that same time in your announcements do not fail to show yourself doubly diplomatic, and make as sure as possible that firm local Soviet authority has been prepared. The same applies to Georgia, although in regard to her I advise even greater circumspection."[27]

Azerbaijan, in accordance with Lenin's instructions, was the first to be retaken. After having laid the groundwork through communist penetration and sedition, the Red Army marched into Baku on April 27,

1920 and took the city without firing a shot. Armenian independence was snuffed out later that year when the Soviet Union and the Armenian Republic signed a treaty at Erevan on December 2, 1920, which transformed it into a Soviet republic.

After having disposed of Azerbaijan, Ordzhonikidze was anxious to move on to Tiflis, but his request for permission to do so was refused. At that very time war had broken out with Poland, which was now, with the help of anticommunist Ukrainian nationalist troops, marching on Kiev. As noted by Richard Pipes, "the prospect of a second front against the relatively well-organized and patriotically inspired Georgians was the last thing the Soviet government desired."[28] Accordingly, the Politburo promptly passed a resolution "immediately to send Ordzhonikidze a telegram in the name of Lenin and Stalin forbidding him to 'self-determine' Georgia, and instructing him to continue negotiations with the Georgian government."[29] On May 7, 1920 a Soviet-Georgian treaty was signed in Moscow that stated, in part:

On the basis of the right of all peoples freely to dispose of themselves up to and including complete separation from the state of which they constitute a part—a right proclaimed by the Socialist Federative Republic of Soviet Russia— Russia recognizes without reservations the independence and the sovereignty of the Georgian state, and renounces of its own will all the sovereign rights which had appertained to Russia with regard to the people and territory of Georgia.

On the basis of the principle proclaimed in the first article of the present treaty, Russia obliges itself to desist from all interference in the internal affairs of Georgia.[30]

Before the ink on the treaty was dry, a secret mission of some 300 agents was sent as a fifth column into Georgia. When it became known, the British foreign secretary, Lord Curzon, protested to Moscow. The response by the Soviet commissar for foreign affairs, Chicherin, was: "Russia has recognized the independence of Georgia. Russian policy supports the principle of self-determination of small nations . . . we have made no demands on Georgia . . . Soviet Russia has not committed and will not commit in future any hostile acts against the Republic of Georgia."[31] As Chicherin sent his telegram, Russian troops were being placed in position for a five-pronged attack on Georgia that took place on Februry 11, 1921. On March 16 the Georgian legislature met for the last time and went into exile to continue the struggle.

Iran

The first serious effort to conquer Persia was mounted by Peter the Great in 1715, when Russia occupied the cities of Derbent and Baku on the western shore of the Caspian Sea. This, in conjunction with Russian moves in Central Asia, led to war with Persia in 1722. By the peace agreement of 1723, Russia received from the weak Shah Talmasp II all the Persian provinces on the shore of the Caspian. Under the shah's successor, however, Persia reneged, and the Russian occupation was thwarted. At the same time, after the death of Peter, the Russian government renounced its claims to the territories because of the expense of defending them. What would later become Russian Azerbaijan was retroceded to Persia between 1729 and 1735. For Peter, Persia was just a way stop on the road to India. Indeed, one of Peter's contemporaries is reported to have said regarding Peter's imperialist policy, "The hopes of His Majesty were not concerned with Persia alone; if he had been lucky in Persia and were still living, he would of course have attempted to reach India or even China."[32]

In the early nineteenth century, through a variety of means of coercion, including force and subversion, Russia realized substantial territorial gains at Persian expense. Russian victories were indemnified by the treaties of Gulistan (1813) and Turkmanchai (1828), both of which involved title to considerable chunks of territory, granted special trade rights, and forfeited Persia's right to maintain a fleet in the Caspian. The latter treaty, in the view of A. Lobanov-Rostovski, marked "the beginning of Russian economic and political penetration of that country"[33] and brought to an end the seizure of Persian territory except for minor border rectifications. In 1869 another Russo-Persian agreement set the lower Atrek River as the common border east of the Caspian Sea.

A major factor that brought about the cessation of the Russian advance into Persia was the deterioration of Anglo-Russian relations subsequent to the appointment of Palmerston as British foreign secretary in 1830. He held the view that any further Russian penetration of Central Asia was a direct threat to British interests in India. This forced the Russians to move more cautiously in the region in order to avoid a direct conflict with Great Britain. This consideration helped shape Russian policy toward Persia for the rest of the century. Imperial policy now required a more sophisticated approach designed to transform Persia incrementally into a Russian protectorate. This may be seen quite clearly in the instruction issued toward the end of the century by the Russian foreign minister, Count Lamsdorff, to his minister in Persia.

The principal aim pursued by us . . . through various ways and means during long years of our relations with Persia can be defined in the following manner: to preserve the integrity and inviolability of the Shah; without seeking for ourselves territorial acquisitions, without permitting the hegemony of a third power, gradually to subject Persia to our dominant influence without violating the external symbols of her independence or her internal regime. In other words, our task is to make Persia politically an obedient and useful ally, a sufficiently powerful instrument in our hands.[34]

It is interesting that, at about the same time as Count Lamsdorff was issuing his instruction, Lord Curzon was warning his countrymen not to be deceived about Russian ambitions in Persia and beyond.

Russia regards Persia as a power that may temporarily be tolerated, that may even require sometimes to be humoured or caressed, but that in the long run is irretrievably doomed. She regards the future partition of Persia as a project scarcely less certain of fulfillment than the achieved partition of Poland; and she has already clearly made up her own mind as to the share which she will require in the division of the spoils. It would be safe to assert that no Russian statesman or officer of the General Staff would pen a report upon Russian policy towards Persia and the future of that country that did not involve as a major premise the Russian annexation of the provinces of Azerbaijan, Gilan, Mazanderan and Khorasan—in other words, of the whole of North Persia, from west to east . . . Russia's appetite for territorial aggrandisement does not stop here. Not content with a spoil that would rob Persia at one sweep of the entire northern half of her dominions, she turns a longing eye southwards, and yearns for an outlet upon the Persian Gulf and the Indian Ocean.[35]

On August 31, 1907, Russia and Great Britain entered into an agreement that effectively partitioned the country between their two zones of interest. Russian forces intervened politically in 1908; and in 1914, because of the outbreak of World War I, they found a rationale for occupying the northern part of the country. When the monarchy was toppled in 1917, Russian forces withdrew but soon returned in the guise of volunteers from Soviet Azerbaijan.

The Soviet heirs of Russian imperialism continued to attach great strategic importance to Persia, both geopolitically and ideologically.

Persia, it was believed, was the vehicle for the revolutionary transformation of all of Asia. Thus, Konstantin Troyanovsky, writing as early as 1918, stated: "The Persian revolution may become the key to the revolution of the whole Orient, just as Egypt and the Suez Canal are the key to English domination in the Orient. Persia is the 'Suez Canal' of the revolution. . . . The political conquest of Persia, thanks to its peculiar geopolitical situation . . . is what we must accomplish first of all. . . . Persia must be ours!"[36]

Beginning in the spring of 1919, Persia served as a springboard for British and White Russian intervention in the Caucasus during the civil war in Russia. After the defeat of Denikin and the reoccupation of Baku in May 1920, the Soviet fleet captured the Persian port of Enzeli and became entrenched in the province of Gilan, which was proclaimed an independent republic the following month. Interestingly, this step, taken on Stalin's initiative, drew a rebuke from Lenin at a meeting of the Politburo. Lenin was concerned that Soviet actions in Gilan would spur the British to remain in Persia and proceed with their idea of a south Persian federation. This would ultimately make it more difficult for the Soviets to consolidate their position in Central Asia. Furthermore, it would exacerbate relations with Britain at a time when the Kremlin was negotiating for loans in London to help rehabilitate Soviet industry.[37] Accordingly, it was decided to surrender Gilan for the sake of broader Soviet interests.

Under the terms of the Soviet-Persian treaty of February 26, 1921, the Persian government regained control over the province. However, the treaty also provided that the Soviet Union would assist Persia if it were to be attacked from the direction of Turkey, and Soviet forces were empowered to enter the country temporarily if it were once again to become a base for hostile activities against the Soviet Union. Presumably, this provision was intended as a hedge against the possibility that Britain might establish a base in south Persia. Soviet troops withdrew in May-June 1921, and Persian troops occupied the "republic" a few months later.[38] The treaty, however, was not ratified by Persia until January 31, 1928, some two weeks after the Soviets also returned the port of Enzeli, which they had continued to occupy.

During the Molotov-Hitler negotiations of November 1940, a long-term delineation of respective spheres of interest was proposed by Germany. Von Ribbentrop suggested that "the focal points in the territorial aspirations of the Soviet Union would presumably be centered south of the territory of the Soviet Union in the direction of the Indian Ocean."[39] On November 26, Molotov advised the German ambassador, Schulenburg, in Moscow that the proposal was acceptable subject to certain conditions, one of which read, "Provided that the area south of Batum and Baku in the general direction of the Persian Gulf is recognized as the center of the aspirations of the Soviet Union."[40]

During World War II the Soviet Union, Great Britain, and the United States established lines of communication through Iran to keep supplies flowing to the Soviet forces on the eastern front. It was understood by the Allied Powers that their presence in Iran conferred no territorial rights there. On August 25, 1941, Moscow made the following formal commitment: "The basis underlying all the treaties and agreements of the Soviet Government is the inviolable principles of respect for the independence and territorial integrity of Iran. After elimination of the danger in question, the Soviet Government undertakes immediately to withdraw its troops from the confines of Persia."[41]

This undertaking to respect the territorial integrity and the sovereignty of Iran was reaffirmed in the Tripartite Treaty of January 29, 1942, the Tehran Agreement of November 1943, and also at the Potsdam Conference in the summer of 1945. Nonetheless, this commitment was systematically and continually violated by the Soviets from the moment of the arrival of their forces on Iranian soil. Within a few months, Moscow was demanding oil and mineral concessions as well as certain political rights in northern Iran.

The northwestern Iranian province of Azerbaijan provided a target of considerable strategic value for the Soviets, and it soon became the target of a Soviet-inspired separatist revolt led by communists. Located at the junction of the Soviet Union, Turkey, and Iraq, under Soviet control it would have driven a wedge between Turkey and Iran, providing ready access to western Turkey through the road to Erzurum. It would also have positioned Soviet forces on the Iraq frontier only about 100 miles from the Kirkuk and Mosul oil fields.[42]

The Soviets took over the press in the north and used it to attack the Iranian government. Well-known communists such as Pishevari, Jaafar, and Javid were brought in and were soon given control of the regional government. On August 26, 1945, Pishevari and the Tudeh party took control of the city of Tabriz, under the protection of Soviet troops. All communications with Teheran were cut off, and forces sent by the central government to restore order were blocked by the Soviets. On

November 24, 1945 the United States sent a note questioning the role of Soviet forces in preventing Teheran from reasserting its authority in Azerbaijan. In its response, the Soviet government denied that it was interfering with the movement of Iranian military and gendarme forces operating in the north, but it went on to say, "The Soviet Government opposed the dispatch of new Iranian troops to northern districts of Iran and informed the Iranian Government that the dispatch of further Iranian forces to northern Iran could cause not the cessation, but the increase, of disorders and likewise bloodshed, which would compel the Soviet Government to introduce into Iran further forces of its own for the purpose of preserving order and of insuring the security of the Soviet garrison."[43]

On December 12, 1945 the Autonomous Republic of Azerbaijan was proclaimed in Tabriz, with Pishevari as prime minister. Three days later the Kurdish People's Republic was set up under Soviet auspices in western Azerbaijan.

The Soviets had maintained an interest in the Kurdish problem since the early 1920s. The traditional homeland of the Kurds straddled the borders of Turkey, Iran, and Iraq and was thus strategically located for the purposes of spreading Soviet influence throughout the Middle East. Furthermore, the route to the Persian Gulf from the Soviet Union passed through Kurdistan. The Kremlin had even toyed with the idea of establishing an autonomous Kurdish republic within the Soviet Union in 1927, as a vehicle for promoting the Kurdish independence movements in Turkey, Iran, and Iraq.[44]

During the war years, Iranian Kurdistan was under Soviet occupation. This presented an opportunity to lay the groundwork for a pro-Soviet autonomy movement. However, the approach to the Kurds had to be handled differently. The communist-dominated Tudeh party had little following in Kurdistan. It was thus incapable of serving as the instrument for galvanizing the Kurds for effective political action. On the other hand, the indigenous Kurdish Komala was too nationalistic for Soviet purposes. Accordingly, in September 1945 the khans of the most important Kurdish tribes were invited by the Soviet commander to a meeting in Tabriz. Upon arrival, the Kurdish leaders were bundled onto a train and taken to Baku in the Soviet Union. There they were harangued by Jafar Bagirov, the head of the Communist party of Soviet Azerbaijan, and were persuaded to organize a new Democratic party to liberate the Kurds under Soviet sponsorship. Shortly thereafter, the Democratic party was duly organized under the leadership of a respected tribal and religious leader, Qazi Mohammed, who promptly declared Kurdistan to be autonomous. On December 15 the diminutive Kurdish People's Republic was established in the towns of Mahabad, Bokan, Maqadeh, and Ushnuyeh.[45]

A few days later in Moscow, U.S. Secretary of State James F. Byrnes confronted Stalin on the matter of the continued presence and actions of Soviet forces in northern Iran. Stalin insisted that under the Persian-Soviet Treaty of 1921, the Soviet Union had the right to send troops into Iran if there were a threat to Soviet security emanating from the country. Byrnes later wrote: "The more I thought about Generalissimo Stalin's excuse for retaining troops in Iran, the less confidence I had in the Soviet position. It was absurd to claim as he had, that the Red Army of 30,000 well-trained and fully equipped troops must stop the poorly trained and inadequately equipped Iranian force of 1,500 from marching toward Azerbaijan on the public highway because it feared a disturbance would be created. . . . And his admission that the question of withdrawal would be examined on the evacuation date showed that our worries about his fulfilling the Teheran declaration were justified.''[46]

Soviet forces, as anticipated, were not removed from Iran as agreed, and the issue was soon brought before the United Nations Security Council over Soviet objections. The continued Soviet occupation of northern Iran was leading to a Soviet-U.S. confrontation, as President Truman became increasingly disturbed over Soviet behavior. It soon became clear to Stalin that he would have to relinquish direct control in Iran in the face of the adamant U.S. stance on the issue. Stalin could not afford the risk of a showdown confrontation with Truman. The U.S. president was, after all, the man who decided to use atomic weapons to force Japan to the surrender table less than a year earlier, and who now seemed intent on getting the Soviets to withdraw from Iran. Nevertheless, the Soviets wished to be sure that the political arrangements they had set up in the north remained intact after their departure, and that they at least reap some economic advantages as part of the price of their withdrawal. This led to a good deal of maneuvering and negotiations.

The agreement worked out by Iranian Prime Minister Qavam pledged to grant the Soviets a major oil concession in return for their withdrawal. His commitment was made subject to the approval of a new *Majlis* (parliament). However, he made clear that the elections for the *Majlis* could not take place while the north was under Soviet occupation. It was thus in the Soviet interest to withdraw its forces sooner rather than later.[47] Soviet troops were finally pulled out on May 9, 1946, leaving behind their puppet governments in Azerbaijan and Mahabad. To Moscow's chagrin, the *Majlis* refused to ratify the oil concession, and in December 1946 the Iranian government reasserted its authority in northern Iran, bringing an end to the two people's republics.

Notes

1. Cited by William G. Bray, *Russian Frontiers: From Muscovy to Khrushchev*, p. 63.
2. Gladys S. Thomson, *Catherine the Great and the Expansion of Russia*, p. 103.
3. B. H. Sumner, *Peter the Great and the Emergence of Russia*, p. 35.
4. Warren B. Walsh, *Russia and the Soviet Union*, p. 205.
5. Ibid., p. 206.
6. Ibid., pp. 206–7.
7. Ibid., p. 209.
8. Graham Stephenson, *Russia from 1812 to 1945*, p. 250.
9. Aaron S. Klieman, *Soviet Russia and the Middle East*, p. 33.
10. *Documents on International Affairs, 1936*, pp. 645–48.
11. Ferenc A. Vali, *The Turkish Straits and NATO*, pp. 35–36.
12. D. A. Routh, *Survey for 1936*, p. 617.
13. Altemur Kiliç, *Turkey and the World*, pp. 78–79.
14. Cited by J. C. Hurewitz, *Diplomacy in the Near and Middle East: A Documentary Record, 1914–1956*, vol. 2, pp. 228–29.
15. Ibid., p. 230.
16. Ferenc A. Vali, *Bridge across the Bosporus*, p. 171.
17. U.S. Department of State, *The Conferences at Malta and Yalta, 1945*, pp. 903–5.
18. Kiliç, op. cit., pp. 125–26.
19. Cited by Bruce R. Kuniholm, *The Origins of the Cold War in the Near East*, p. 297.
20. U.S. Department of State, *The Problem of the Turkish Straits*, pp. 47–49.
21. Ibid., pp. 50–55.
22. Vali, *Bridge*, p. 193.
23. *Documents on International Affairs, 1953*, pp. 277–78.
24. Duygu Bazoglu Sezer, "Turkey's Security Policies," in Jonathan Alford, ed., *Greece and Turkey: Adversity in Alliance*, p. 58.

25. Boris Nolde, *La formation de l'Empire Russe*, p. 307.
26. Ibid., p. 318.
27. Cited by Pipes, op. cit., p. 224.
28. Ibid., p. 227.
29. Ibid.
30. Ibid., p. 228.
31. Cited by Bray, op. cit., p. 72.
32. George Vernadsky, *A History of Russia*, p. 104.
33. A. Lobanov-Rostovski, *Russia and Asia*, p. 111.
34. Cited by Firuz Kazemzadeh, "Russia and the Middle East," in Ivo J. Lederer, ed., *Russian Foreign Policy: Essays in Historical Perspective*, p. 509.
35. George N. Curzon, *Persia and the Persian Question*, vol. 2, pp. 593–97.
36. Cited by Ivan Spector, *The Soviet Union and the Muslim World 1917–1958*, pp. 84–85.
37. Louis Fischer, *Russia's Road from Peace to War*, p. 63.
38. Max Beloff, *The Foreign Policy of Soviet Russia*, vol. 2, pp. 200–201.
39. R. J. Sontag and J. S. Beddie, eds., *Nazi-Soviet Relations, 1939–1941: Documents from the Archives of the German Foreign Office*, p. 250.
40. Cited by Hurewitz, op. cit., p. 230.
41. Cited by Bray, op. cit., p. 64.
42. Jules Menken, "Britain and the Persian Question," *National Review*, January 1946, pp. 26–27.
43. *New York Times*, December 9, 1945.
44. Gunther Nollau and Hans J. Wiehe, *Russia's South Flank*, p. 52.
45. Ibid., pp. 53–57.
46. James F. Byrnes, *Speaking Frankly*, p. 119.
47. Faramarz S. Fatemi, *The U.S.S.R. in Iran*, pp. 174–75.

4 Expansion in Central Asia

Southeast of the Ural Mountains, between the Caspian Sea, the Ural River, and the Chinese frontier, lie the steppes of Central Asia. Farther to the south, between the steppes and the Iranian and Afghan frontiers, at the end of the Silk Road from China, lie the ancient centers of Central Asian culture and trade, which were ruled by the khans of Khiva and Bokhara. Early Russian attempts to penetrate into the lands of Central Asia met with the resolute opposition of the fiercely independent Kazakh, Kalmuk, and Turkoman hordes that roamed the region. Preoccupied with the struggles in Europe and the march across Siberia, the czars were unable to devote the necessary attention and resources to this region. As a consequence, during the earliest phases of Russian imperial expansion in Asia, the troublesome steppe region was bypassed. Russian contacts with the commercial centers of the south were restricted to an occasional caravan.

At the beginning of the eighteenth century, however, conditions appeared to be right for a new and more serious Russian drive southward in this sector. The Kalmuks, who were at the time the most powerful horde on the steppes, were being pushed westward by the Chinese, who were attempting to solidify their control over Mongolia and Xinjiang in reaction to Russian pressures on those regions of the Manchu empire.

In turn, the Kalmuks were incrementally displacing the Kazakhs, who squeezed the khanates to the south, particularly Bokhara. The latter had reached and passed its peak and was now engaged in incessant squabbling with neighboring Khiva. In both 1700 and 1703, Peter I received appeals from the khan of Khiva for help against Bokhara.[1]

Notwithstanding the rumors that started to circulate about gold deposits in Central Asia, Peter was too preoccupied with his war with Sweden to respond favorably. However, when a similar appeal was received a decade later, Peter decided to wait no longer. His plan was ambitious and perhaps overly simplistic. A large expedition was to penetrate Central Asia to explore the region, search out any sources of gold, and establish trade relations with the local centers. If possible, both Khiva and Bokhara were to be subjugated and brought under the czar's suzerainty. Finally, a detachment was to be sent up the Oxus to establish a link into India.[2] Peter was unaware, however, that the request from Khiva for Russian protection was not intended seriously. Presumably, its purpose was to worry Bokhara enough to reduce its pressure on Khiva.

In 1715 a preliminary expedition entered the Kazakh Steppe, following the Irtysh and Erket rivers, establishing Omsk on the former the following year. In 1717 the major expedition was undertaken, but it proceeded from a different direction. A 6,655-man force was transported to the eastern shore of the Caspian Sea and then crossed the desert from there to Khiva. To the Khivans, this Russian force was correctly seen as a threat to their security. The Russians were split up into small groups, ostensibly to facilitate the provision of quarters for them, and then massacred. Those who escaped died in the desert for the most part. There were only a few who made it back to Russia. Peter experienced this setback primarily because he acted precipitately, sending a force to conquer a territory without first securing his lines of communication and establishing defensible forward positions. The struggle for Central Asia was to be long and hard fought.

The mistakes of 1717 were not to be repeated. Future penetration of Central Asia would be pursued from forward positions with secure lines to the rear. In addition to Omsk, in 1716, Semipalatinsk was established farther upstream to the south on the Irtysh River in 1718. This was followed by the founding of the additional fortified posts of Orsk and Orenburg on the Ural River in 1735 and 1743. Orenburg was to serve as the main base for the subsequent conquest of Central Asia.

In 1731 the Kazakhs of the Lesser Horde, followed in 1740 by some of the Middle Horde, were forced to accept nominal Russian suzerainty, although it took another 80 years to bring them firmly under control. This extended Russia's reach as far south as the Aral Sea. At the turn of the century, Paul I, in conjunction with his new alliance with Napoleon, dispatched an expedition of 22,500 Don Cossacks from Orenburg to march through Khiva and Bokhara and to attack the British in India.[3] Although the scheme collapsed with the czar's assassination and a subsequent reorientation of Russian policy, it raised a concern for the security of northern India that contributed to the tension in Anglo-Russian relations in Central Asia for more than a century afterward.

Actual pacification of the region began only with the well-organized drive to the south that started in the nineteenth century under Alexander I. In 1822 the khanate of the Middle Horde was abolished and its lands carved up. Russian suzerainty was now transformed into sovereignty. In 1824 the relative independence of the Lesser Horde was similarly eliminated, bringing about a series of revolts in 1827–29 and over the period 1832–38. The Russian drive, however, could not be stopped by the remaining independent Kazakh hordes, which were subjugated around 1847, when the Greater Horde capitulated and offered its allegiance to the czar. Richard A. Pierce wrote of the struggle:

The Kazakhs, numerous but disunited, courageous but ill-armed, were no match for their more advanced foes. Using a bag of tricks developed through long experience in border warfare—negotiation, bribery, blandishment, and patronage of the weak and subversion of the strong—the Russians moved ahead to new positions, set up defense lines and consolidated gains during times when they were occupied elsewhere, then moved on again when they were ready. It is no wonder that the succession of the Russian acquisitions in this region appeared to some foreign observers as a result of a long-standing Grand Design.[4]

With the incorporation of the lands of the Greater Kazakh Horde, the frontier of the Russian empire in Central Asia ran from the Caspian through the Aral Sea to the Kuldzha region of Xinjiang. Now, for the first time, Russia was well positioned to throw its weight against the Uzbek khanates of Kokand, Khiva, and Bokhara to the south. The conquest was long and bitterly resisted. One of the stratagems employed by the Russians in the fierce struggle was unabashed terror, most notably in the pursuit and massacre of the Turkomen in 1881. The perception

62   *The Strategy of Soviet Imperialism*

underlying the use of this savage approach was articulated by the Russian general M. D. Skobelev, who stated, "I hold it as a principle that in Asia the duration of peace is in direct proportion to the slaughter you inflict upon the enemy. The harder you hit them the longer they will be quiet afterwards."[5]

The conquest was delayed in part because of the nature of the terrain. Since much of the area was desert, there was a continuing necessity to establish forward bases and to secure the lines of communication to the rear.[6] Ak-Mechet (Perovsk), on the Syr-Darya River in northwestern Kokand, was taken in 1853. The following year the Russians founded Alma-Ata on the Kazakh side of the frontier. The pace of the Russian movement was slow and deliberate. It took another decade of such preparations before the conquest of Kokand, to be followed by the other khanates, could be undertaken. One of the significant economic incentives that spurred the Russians to accelerate their efforts at the beginning of the 1860s came as a consequence of the Civil War in the United States. Between 1861 and 1864 the price of Turkestan cotton jumped by 500–600 percent.[7]

The official Russian interpretation of imperial policy in Central Asia was first articulated in a dispatch to Russian representatives abroad by the foreign minister, Prince A. M. Gorchakov, on December 3, 1864. Gorchakov stated:

The position of Russia in Central Asia is that of all civilized States which are brought into contact with half savage, nomad populations, possessing no fixed social organization.

In such cases it always happens that the more civilized State is forced, in the interests of the security of its frontier and its commercial relations, to exercise a certain ascendancy over those whom their turbulent and unsettled character makes most undesirable neighbours.

First there are raids and acts of pillage to put down. To put a stop to them, the tribes on the frontier have to be reduced to a state of more or less perfect submission.[8]

The implication of Gorchakov's argument was that these sorts of problem were endemic because there existed a power vacuum in the region that was inherently destabilizing. It was thus necessary for Russia to fill the void because it was the state most directly affected by its consequences.

The capital of Kokand, Tashkent, fell to the Russians in 1865, and peace was negotiated in 1868. Under the terms of the peace accord, Kokand became a protectorate. When it was subsequently annexed in 1876, the imperial proclamation declared, "We, Alexander II, etc., yielding to the wishes of the Khokandi people to become Russian subjects, and likewise recognizing the absolute impossibility of restoring the Khanate to peace and tranquility by any other means, command that the Khanate of Khokand be immediately incorporated within our dominions and that it shall henceforth form the 'Fergana province' of our Empire."[9]

In 1865, in anticipation of what awaited it once the Russians disposed of Kokand, Bokhara sent its forces to attack the Russians while they were still preoccupied with its conquest. But it was already too late. The Russian drive could no longer be stopped. In May 1866, Russian forces moved against Bokhara. When the British, concerned about the possible implications of the Russian approach toward India, inquired as to the proposed limits of the Russian advance, Gorchakov responded that it was a purely military decision, and that, in any case, it didn't pose any threat to India. Firuz Kazemzadeh has observed: "The pattern was now established. Year after year Russian troops would penetrate deeper into the heart of Asia. A flurry of alarm would run from Calcutta, or Simla, to Whitehall. The British ambassador in St. Petersburg would call on Russia's minister of foreign affairs, ask for an explanation, receive assurances of the tsar's determination not to annex an inch of land anywhere, send a dispatch to that effect to Her Majesty's Principal Secretary for Foreign Affairs, and leave the matter there until Russia's next move reopened the whole issue."[10]

The Bokharan capital and Samarkand fell in 1868, and a peace agreement was concluded the same year. Russia annexed Samarkand and the adjacent areas, while the remainder of Bokhara became a protectorate. It retained that status until 1917. Khiva, the least accessible of the Central Asian khanates, was the last to succumb. Russian preparations for the final assault were completed by 1873, and Khiva, the capital, soon fell. Under the terms of the peace agreement, all Khivan territory on the north bank of the Amu-Darya River was annexed, and Khiva became a protectorate and retained that status until 1917. The annexed territories of the three khanates were incorporated into the governor-generalship of Turkestan, which had been set up in 1867 with headquarters at Tashkent.

Between 1881 and 1885, Russia conquered, with great brutality, as was noted earlier, the Turkoman settlements south of the Kara-Kum Desert. This campaign was successful only after the completion of a railroad eastward from Krasnovodsk on the Caspian, which facilitated the isolation of the Turkoman stronghold at Gheok Tepe. Skobolev took the city in January 1881 and authorized the slaughter of all male Turkomans, an orgy of killing that took place over a four-day period.[11] The railroad was then extended as far as Kizil Arvat, about 145 miles inland from the Caspian, by the end of 1881. It is estimated that during the reign of Alexander II (1855–81), some 400,000 square miles of territory in Central Asia were added to the Russian empire.

Soviet revisionist historians would later attempt to demonstrate that the Russian penetration of Central Asia was not inherently motivated by expansionist aims. It was, it would be argued, essentially a self-defense measure provoked by British attempts to expand their empire in India to include these regions close to the Russian frontier. In this regard, it is of interest to note the rationale for the Russian advance provided in 1884 by General Leonid Sobolev. Sobolev was of the school that maintained that the principal goal of Russian foreign policy was to expel the Turks from Europe and assume control of the straits linking the Black Sea and the Mediterranean. The achievement of this goal, however, was being successfully opposed by the British. Thus it became necessary to apply pressure against the British in a region of even greater interest to them, namely Afghanistan and India. The greater the threat to India, the more would British power be drawn away from Turkey and the Near East. Sobolev wrote: "It has now become perfectly clear that England and Russia have entered the lists as . . . rivals on the Asiatic continent. England gave the first provocation when she threw down the gauntlet under the walls of Sebastopol [the Crimean War]. We boldly, though sorrowfully, accepted the challenge, and if Russian standards are displayed on the banks of the Syr-Daria and the Oxus, and at Merv, and if the points of Russian bayonets glisten in the neighbourhood of Herat and the Hindu-Kush it is to the English themselves that this is due. It is the British who have impelled us into Asia."[12]

What this rationalization neglects to account for, of course, are the Russian attempts to penetrate Central Asia for more than 200 years, a program that was initiated long before the British were in a position to block their ambitions in Turkey. Indeed, only a few years before Sobolev wrote, an article appeared in the *Moscow Gazette* (July 19, 1878) that stated, "The time has arrived for Russia to establish her influence over the whole of Central Asia, and this is all the more easy as the ruler of Afghanistan is not on good terms with the British—our foe in Central Asia.''[13] Nonetheless, the apologetic approach does demonstrate sound strategic thinking in continental terms. Russia's advance toward the Afghan frontier and India could indeed be used to apply leverage on Britain's policy in the Near East. Indeed, the contemporary buildup of Soviet power in the Far East, as will be discussed later, to a large extent serves comparable strategic purposes.

The capture of Merv in 1884 triggered widespread alarm among Britain's India experts. One of them wrote at that time:

The conquest of Merv is something more than annexation of a sand-desert oasis. It means the complete junction of the military forces of the Caucasus and Turkestan. It means, with the annexation of Akhal, the absorption of 100,000 of the best irregular cavalry in the world, at a week's march from the city of Herat. It means the meeting, for the first time, of the Cossack and the Afghan. It means the complete closure of Khiva within the Russian Empire, and the reduction of Bukhara from the independent position of a border State to the dependence of an incorporated province. It means the enclosure of more than 200,000 square miles of territory, and the addition to the Russian Empire of a region as large as France. It means the completion of the conquest of the Central Asian deserts, and the commencement of the annexation of the great fertile mountain region of Persia and Afghanistan. It means the deliberate occupation of a strategical point, fraught with political entanglements of such a widespread nature that, whether Russia desire it or not, she will be inevitably led, unless forestalled or checked by England, to Meshed, to Herat, to Balkh, and to Kabul. And she will not remain there. She will continue her swift advance until she triumphantly lays down her Cossack border alongside the Sepoy line of India.[14]

In retrospect, this analysis was remarkably prescient except, as might be expected, with regard to the element of timing. It took almost 100 years before a Russian army was to be headquartered in Kabul.

In 1885 the Russians engaged and defeated an Afghan force at Ak Tepe in the Penjdeh Oasis region along the Afghan frontier. This generated a new crisis with Great Britain, which saw the incident as evidence of Russian intentions to penetrate Afghanistan and threaten India. However, at the time, neither Russia nor Britain was prepared to go to war over an Afghan village. Accordingly, the British redrew the frontier, awarding Penjdeh to Russia. This completed the Russian conquest of Central Asia and fixed, except for minor negotiated revisions, the approximately 600-mile-long border with Persia east of the Caspian Sea. The brazenness of Russian expansionism in Central Asia and the complacency with which it was accepted is well captured in the letter sent to the London *Times* on March 19, 1885 by Sir Edward Hamley. He stated, in part:

Our manner of meeting [Russia] is among the marvels of the most unaccountable period of her history. We treat her as one of two established conterminous powers whose respective limits require definition. The facts are dropped out of sight that a few years ago she was a thousand miles from the Afghan frontier, and that she grounds her brand new title to contest its territory with us, on her conquest of certain predatory tribes on whose outskirts other predatory tribes wander, and that on the strength of this extraordinary claim she suddenly puts forth the impudent formula, "Whatever territory you cannot satisfactorily prove your right to is mine," which henceforth becomes the basis of of negotiations.[15]

The crisis with Britain spurred the Russians on to completing the Transcaspian Railway, which reached Samarkand in 1888. A branch line between Merv and Kushk was seen in British India as a possible military threat aimed at Herat, and it caused some concern about Russian intentions. Nonetheless, the completion of the Transcaspian did not lead to an Anglo-Russian conflict in Central Asia. Both sides tacitly acknowledged that a balance of power had been reached in the region.[16]

Afghanistan

In 1895, Russia added the remote area of Pamir near the Indian frontier to its empire. Only the panhandle of the Wakhan Valley now separated Russia from British India, a situation that was to the liking of neither. The two imperial powers agreed to establish a neutral buffer zone between their empires that would be offered to Afghanistan. The Anglo-Russian Pamir Boundary Commission of 1895 delineated the Wakhan corridor, which at one point is as narrow as 8 miles. Its eastern boundary with China, finally demarcated by the Afghans and the Chinese in 1964, is about 50 miles long. Amir Abdur Rahman, the ruler of Afghanistan at the time, wanted no part of the inhospitable Wakhan, which he declared was like a long arm "which could be shorn off by the Russians whenever they pleased." He was convinced that the Russians intended to invade India and that Afghanistan lay in their path. Later, he wrote in his memoirs, "There is not the slightest doubt that

Russia is determined and certain in her heart to attack India whenever she finds an opportunity to do so."[17] Abdur Rahman agreed to incorporate the Wakhan into Afghanistan only after the British agreed to pay him an additional annual subsidy. The rest of the Russo-Afghan border was negotiated for the most part by Great Britain in 1873, 1885, and 1895, without consulting Afghanistan.

After the Russian revolution, steps were taken as early as the spring of 1919 to establish relations between the Soviet Union and Afghanistan. Lenin wrote to Amanullah, "Convinced that the friendship between Russia and Afghanistan will henceforth continue to grow in strength, I take the liberty of expressing to you my sympathetic feeling and my conviction that the independence of the great Afghan State will never be violated, either by force or by stratagem."[18]

After the Soviets restored order in Central Asia, where an insurrection broke out in Bokhara in 1920, an Afghan-Soviet treaty of friendship and alliance was signed on February 28, 1921. From the Soviet perspective, the treaty created the opportunity to use Afghanistan as a base for promoting revolution in India. Indian revolutionaries were sent by the Soviets to Kabul, where they were permitted to establish a "Provisional Government of the People of India." Plans were also drawn up to organize and train an "Indian Liberation Army" in Afghanistan. Joseph Surits, the Soviet ambassador in Kabul, reportedly sent agents to the Pushtun tribes along the Indian frontier in an effort to get them to harass the British.[19]

As the process of Sovietization began to take place in Central Asia in 1924–25, tensions grew along the Soviet-Afghan border over the question of sovereignty over Urta-Tagai, a small island in the Oxus River. An armed clash occurred in December 1925. The Soviets moved to defuse the crisis, and on August 31, 1926 the two countries signed a treaty of neutrality and nonaggression. The pro-Soviet government of Amanullah was subsequently ousted by a revolt that broke out after he returned from a visit to Moscow in the summer of 1928. Although the Soviets intervened briefly on behalf of the king, they soon withdrew. The rebel government of Habibullah Khan was in turn overthrown in 1929 by Nadir Shah who restored the monarchy that October, when he was proclaimed king. The Soviets intervened in Afghanistan again in June 1930, when they crossed the Oxus in pursuit of Ibrahim Beg, one of the last of the leaders of the Basmachi revolt in Soviet Turkestan. On June 31, 1931 a new Afghan-Soviet nonaggression pact was signed.

However, the Muslim countries on Russia's southern flank were wary of Soviet ambitions in the region and in 1937 signed the Saadabad Pact, which formed a defensive alliance of Afghanistan, Turkey, Iran, and Iraq. Notwithstanding the Saadabad Pact, Soviet influence increased in Afghanistan with the significant increase of the Soviet share of Afghanistan's foreign trade, which reached 24 percent by 1939.

Though the growth of Soviet influence ceased because of the disruptions caused by World War II, new and significant opportunities presented themselves in the postwar years, especially after the British withdrawal from neighboring India in 1947. Soviet influence began to grow markedly in Afghanistan during the 1950s. This came about by the astute exploitation of the openings unintentionally created for them, albeit indirectly, by the United States.

Afghanistan had become embroiled in a lingering controversy with Pakistan over the question of Pushtunistan. The Pushtuns constitute the largest ethnic group in Afghanistan with some eight million members. There is also an equal number in Pakistan. When the British left India and the North West Frontier Province became part of Pakistan, the Pushtuns of the province were given the choice of joining either India or Pakistan. The Pushtuns, as Muslims, chose Pakistan. Afghanistan, however, believed that they should have been given the option of becoming independent or acceding to Afghanistan, since the province had originally been carved out of Afghan territory. Thus, on June 21, 1947, Afghanistan's Prime Minister Mohammad Hashim Khan stated that "if an independent Pakhtoonistan cannot be set up, the Frontier Province should join Afghanistan." Furthermore, he made it implicitly clear that Afghanistan's concern was not limited to the well-being of ethnic Pushtuns across the border. He also remarked, "Our neighbour will realize that our country, with its population and trade, needs an outlet to the sea, which is very essential."[20] A few days later, the Indian press carried the following observation on the issue: "While there is no evidence to suggest that the Afghan claim on the N.W.F.P. has been inspired by Russia, such a move is clearly in line with Moscow's views on the desirability of uniting natural entities with national frontiers."[21]

Since Pakistan had aligned itself with the West by joining the South East Asia Treaty Organization (SEATO) in 1954, and the Baghdad Pact—later the Central Treaty Organization (CENTO)—in 1955, the Soviets were only too pleased to throw their support behind the Afghans. When Afghanistan persisted in agitation among the Pushtuns, Pakistan closed the border, blocking the transit of its commerce to the sea. This forced Afghanistan to turn to the Soviet Union for an outlet. Then, when the threat of conflict with Pakistan became heightened and Afghanistan turned to the United States for arms, Washington refused to assist it against Pakistan. Once again the Soviets were happy to oblige.

The Pushtunistan issue provided an umbrella under which the Soviets could make significant inroads by overtly supporting Afghan nationalism. The Soviet press began agitating for the creation of a Pushtunistan state that would include all the Pushtu-speaking residents of Pakistan's northwestern province. When Khrushchev and Bulganin visited Afghanistan in December 1955, they signed a mutual declaration with their host that stated, in part, "The government of the U.S.S.R. and the royal Government of Afghanistan are convinced that those peoples and nations who have hitherto been deprived of their liberty and national sovereignty are entitled on the basis of the U.N. statutes to decide their future destiny without any pressure or the exercise thereof from outside.''[22] This position was reaffirmed in more explicit fashion on the occasion of Khrushchev's second visit to Kabul in March 1960, when the communiqué stated, ''Both sides exchanged views on the future of the Pathan people and expressed their agreement that the correct and sensible way to a relaxation of tension and to peace in the Middle East lies in the application to this problem of the principle of self-determination in accordance with the United Nations Charter.''[23] When fighting along the Afghanistan-Pakistan border broke out again in early 1961, the Soviet Union let it be known that the area in dispute between the two countries was so close to the Soviet border that Moscow could not ignore its implications for the stability and security of its territory.[24] This barely veiled warning to Pakistan set the stage for subsequent Soviet involvement in Afghan affairs.

In 1955 the Soviets granted Afghanistan a $100-million line of credit that went mostly for assistance in the development of the country's infrastructure. Included among the development projects supported by the Soviets were highways, bridges, the Bagram airport north of Kabul, and a road through the Salang Pass (originally begun by Soviet engineers in 1927 but stopped because of the 1928 revolt in Afghanistan) connecting the two countries through the Hindu Kush Mountains. Thomas T. Hammond has noted: ''It was probably no accident that the roads and bridges Moscow constructed were strong enough and wide enough to carry the Soviet tanks that invaded Afghanistan two decades later.

Similarly, the Salang tunnel and the chain of supply depots for grain and oil were on the main road used by the invading Soviet army, and the Soviet-built airfields at Shindand and Bagram were important landing sites for the Soviet airborne troops that were flown into Afghanistan in December 1979. Thus the Soviets used their aid program to prepare the way for their subsequent conquest of Afghanistan."[25]

The Russians had long maintained the belief that the natural southern boundary of Soviet Central Asia lay not at the Oxus River at the northern border of the Wakhan corridor, but at the Hindu Kush range along its southern border. The Hindu Kush stretches from the Chinese border across Afghanistan almost to the Iranian border. According to reports emanating from Pakistan in late 1986, it appears that the Afghans agreed in 1980 to a Soviet annexation of the Wakhan strip.[26] If this is indeed the case, it would seem that the Soviets are now well positioned to annex all of Afghanistan north of the Hindu Kush.

Notes

1. B. H. Sumner, *Peter the Great and the Emergence of Russia*, p. 153.
2. Ibid.
3. Michael Rywkin, *Russia in Central Asia*, p. 18.
4. Richard A. Pierce, *Russian Central Asia, 1867–1917*, p. 18.
5. George N. Curzon, *Russia in Central Asia in 1889 and the Anglo-Russian Question*, pp. 85–86.
6. Allen F. Chew, *An Atlas of Russian History*, p. 76.
7. Warren B. Walsh, *Russia and the Soviet Union*, p. 272.
8. Cited by Firuz Kazemzadeh, "Russia and the Middle East," in Ivo J. Lederer, ed., *Russian Foreign Policy*, p. 494.
9. Ibid., pp. 501–2.
10. Ibid., p. 498.
11. Graham Stephenson, *Russia from 1812 to 1945*, pp. 281–82. According to sources cited by Kazemzadeh, op. cit., p. 505, the total killed was 8,000 fugitives—men, women, and children.
12. Cited by Kazemzadeh, op. cit., pp. 495–96.
13. Cited by M. Raziullah Azmi, "Russian Expansion in Central Asia and the Afghan Question (1865–85)," *Pakistan Horizon*, Third Quarter, 1984, p. 124.
14. Charles Marvin, cited by W. P. and Zelda K. Coates, *Soviets in Central Asia*, p. 48.
15. Cited by Alexis Krausse, *Russia in Asia: A Record and a Study, 1558–1899*, p. 240.

16. Stephenson, op. cit., p. 282.

17. Mir Munshi, Sultan Mohammed Khan, ed., *The Life of Abdur Rahman, Amir of Afghanistan*, pp. 260ff.

18. Cited by Guenther Nollau and Hans J. Wiehe, *Russia's South Flank*, pp. 95–96.

19. Harish Kapur, *Soviet Russia and Asia, 1917–1927: A Study of Soviet Policy towards Turkey, Iran and Afghanistan*, pp. 230–33.

20. *Statesman* (Delhi), June 22, 1947.

21. Ibid., July 3, 1947.

22. Cited by Nollau and Wiehe, op. cit., p. 110.

23. Ibid.

24. *Pravda*, March 25, 1961.

25. Thomas T. Hammond, *Red Flag over Afghanistan*, p. 25.

26. William J. Coughlin, "Soviets Quietly Annex Strategic Afghan Turf," *Washington Times*, November 10, 1986.

5   Expansion to the East

Starting from the recently reconstituted Russian state in the region west of the Urals at the end of the sixteenth century, within 100 years the czars' reach extended to the Pacific. The phenomenally rapid expansion across the vast land mass of Asia started without benefit of any clear plan. Indeed, it can be traced to the land grant made by Ivan the Terrible to the Stroganov brothers in 1574. They had requested the grant so that they could exploit the silver and iron deposits that were expected to be found in the region between the Ural Mountains and the Tura and Tobol rivers.[1] The only problem with the czar's generosity was that the land was not his to give. It had to be conquered before the land grant meant much. This task fell to groups of freebooting Cossacks, who crossed the Urals into Siberia in search of furs and precious metals.

Within a few years these hardy groups of pioneers established a chain of fortified outposts across the Vasyugan Plain, starting with Tobolsk in 1587, which were promptly claimed by the czar and incorporated into the Russian empire. With a rudimentary infrastructure already in place as a consequence of these pioneer efforts, the Russians soon began a serious colonization drive eastward across Siberia. They founded new major posts as they went: Kuznetsk in 1618, Yeniseysk in 1619, Krasnoyarsk in 1628, Ilimsk in 1630, and Bratsk in 1631. The advance took place for the most part along a line north of the most populated regions of the continent. As a general rule, the preferred routes skirted the areas that were likely to present significant obstacles to the drive eastward. In particular, the Russians avoided contact whenever possible with the warlike nomadic hordes of the steppes of Central Asia.

The drive eastward encountered virtually no effective opposition until it reached the area just west of Lake Baikal. There it ran into the Buryat Mongols, who blocked the Russian path. Unable to continue eastward along the Mongolian frontier without first overcoming the Buryats and other powerful groups of Mongols, the Russians elected to avoid such confrontations whenever possible, at least for the moment. Instead, they turned northward toward the Lena River Valley, where they established Yakutsk in 1632. From there they moved eastward until they reached the Sea of Okhotsk seven years later. They then turned back to Yakutsk and from there proceeded southward.

Overcoming the opposition of the scattered local populations, they crossed the Stanovoy Mountains and entered the Amur River Basin in 1649. A number of these Russian expeditions were led by Erofei P. Khabarov between 1649 and 1652. The brutal massacres carried out by Khabarov's forces caused the people of the region to appeal for help from the Manchu emperor. The Manchus had supplanted the Ming Dynasty in Beijing in 1644 and were pursuing an expansionist program of their own. As early as 1636 the Manchus had begun making forays into the Amur region from their native Manchuria. The Russians were now competing in an area that the Manchus considered to be within their sphere of interest.

The struggle for control of the Amur Basin continued for some 30 years. During this long period the Russians had succeeded in overcoming the Buryats, and they founded Nerchinsk in 1656–58, Irkutsk in 1661, and Selenginsk in 1666. However, they were unable to make any headway against the Manchus in the Amur region. The fundamental problem was that their lines of communication to the sources of supplies in the west were too extended to enable the Russian forces to sustain the level of effort needed to dislodge the Manchus.

The contest for the Amur Basin was ultimately settled by the Treaty of Nerchinsk (September 7, 1689). Under its terms, which reflected an imprecise knowledge of the geography of the region by both sides, and which are hardly traceable on contemporary maps, the Russians were compelled to withdraw behind the Stanovoy Mountains and were not permitted to make use of the Amur or any of the rivers that flow into the Amur.[2] However, they were compensated by the Manchus with title to some 90,000 square miles of territory.

The Kamchatka peninsula was discovered in 1697, but it was not until 1732 that the determined resistance of the indigenous population was overcome. The naval base of Petropavlovsk was established in 1740 on the southeastern coast. While the slow conquest of Kamchatka was being pursued, groups of Cossacks began the exploration and occupation of the Kurile Islands, starting in about 1711.

The founding of Irkutsk near the southern end of Lake Baikal set the stage for the subsequent and unrelenting Sino-Russian rivalry over Mongolia. The Mongolian steppe lands and desert provide an easy direct route from Siberia to Beijing and the heartland of China. This put the Russians in a strategic position to apply considerable pressure on the Manchu emperors, whereas the latter were unable to pose a comparable threat to the Russian heartland. With the outbreak of a major war with China looming on the horizon, Catherine I took steps to defuse the mounting crisis through diplomacy. In August 1725 she sent an emissary to begin negotiations on the delineation of the border between Siberia and Mongolia. Under the Treaty of Kiakhta (October 31, 1727) the Russians received title to some 40,000 square miles of additional territory south of Lake Baikal between the Sayan Mountains and the Argun River.

Temporarily blocked from further advance in Manchuria and Mongolia, the Russians redirected their attention to projecting southward in western Siberia. They consolidated their grip on the upper reaches of the Yenisei, Ob, and Irtysh rivers. By the end of the century, they achieved control over the Turkic tribes of the Altai region, between Semipalatinsk and western Mongolia. The northwestern boundary of Mongolia was delimited by the extent of these traditional tribal lands.

The Opium War (1840–42) demonstrated the basic weakness of the Manchu regime and encouraged Russia to seek to continue its expansion in the Far East. In 1850, in direct contravention of the Treaty of Nerchinsk, a Russian post was established at Nikolayevsk at the mouth of the Amur, which became the home base of the Russian Pacific fleet. As the Russians were now prepared to invade Manchuria in force, the Chinese were forced to negotiate once again. The Treaty of Aigun (May 28, 1858) yielded to Russia most of the territory north of the Amur between the Aigun and the Pacific. The treaty also provided for joint

Sino-Russian occupation of the region south of the Amur between the Ussuri River and the sea. The net gain for the Russian empire was approximately 170,000 square miles of territory. They then established the town of Khabarovsk, strategically located near the junction of the Amur and the Ussuri. Dissatisfied by the extent of these gains, particularly the provision requiring joint occupancy of the region east of the Ussuri, the Russians succeeded in taking advantage of the weakness of the Chinese government in the face of the Taiping Rebellion to pressure it into further concessions. Under the Treaty of Peking (November 14, 1860) the Sino-Russian border was definitively drawn along the Amur and Ussuri rivers, giving the Russians complete control of the region between the Ussuri and the Pacific. A dozen years later, Russia moved its Pacific fleet headquarters from Nikolayevsk to Vladivostok.

Chinese weakness had also been exploited by the Russians in the west, where they now drove south into Inner Asia as far as the borders of the khanates of Khiva and Bokhara, incorporating these lands into the empire as they went. By 1854 they penetrated into the lower Ili Valley, one of the main routes into Xinjiang from Central Asia. Once again the Russians were in a position to force the Chinese into a negotiation designed to legitimate Russian conquests. The resulting Treaty of Tarbagatai in 1864 established the southwest boundary of Mongolia, ceding the Tien-Shan region to Russia. The boundaries of Siberia, Mongolia, and Xinjiang were finally delimited in 1870 by the Treaty of Uliassutay.

Beijing's hold on Xinjiang, however, was rather tenuous. The Turkic-speaking Muslim populations of the region resented rule by the Chinese and revolted repeatedly throughout the nineteenth century. During one such revolt, which began in the Tarim basin in 1870, under instructions from Saint Petersburg, the governor of Russian Turkestan crossed the border into Xinjiang in 1871 and occupied the upper Ili district, ostensibly to maintain order in an area adjacent to Russian territory. This put the Russians in control of the strategic passes through the mountains in the area and in a position to move into northwest China. By 1875, however, the Chinese had succeeded in suppressing the Muslim revolt and restoring control over the region. The Russians, nonetheless, refused to leave, demanding the cession of the strategic passes as well as the valley of the Tekes River. This the Chinese refused to do.

The Chinese statesman responsible for dealing with the crisis, Tso

Tsung-tang, understood well the strategic implications of the Russian control of the Ili region and preferred war to meeting Russia's demands. He petitioned the emperor for permission to initiate hostilities. His argument was straightforward and highly perceptive. "It seems that Russia intends to make Ili a Russian colony. . . . When a country is defeated in war it may be obliged to cede territory and to sue for peace. But up to the present moment not a single shot has been fired. Why should China sacrifice an important area to satisfy Russia's greed? It would be like throwing a bone to a dog to prevent it from biting. When the bone has been eaten the dog would still want to bite. The loss at present is apparent and the trouble in the future will be endless."[3]

In the face of this determined opposition, the Russians backed off and agreed to withdraw from Ili. However, not without exacting compensation for having given up that which was not theirs in the first place. The Treaty of Saint Petersburg (Februry 24, 1881) awarded the Russians an indemnity of nine million rubles in addition to 18,000 square miles of territory near Lake Zaysan. Nonetheless, the British ambassador to Russia at the time was reported to have said afterward, "China has compelled Russia to do what she has never done before—disgorge territory she had once absorbed."[4]

The growing importance and extent of Russian holdings in Asia demanded a significant improvement of the imperial lines of communication if the empire was to be kept intact and exploited to the advantage of European Russia. The border areas would have to be settled and controlled, and this again would require a modern transportation system. Accordingly, as early as 1855, plans were laid for the Trans-Siberian Railway. Actual construction did not begin for some years: the first section of track, between Vladivostok and Khabarovsk, began to be laid in 1891. From 1892 to 1895 construction proceeded on the line from Chelyabinsk in the Urals eastward to Lake Baikal. In the meantime, in 1895 China was roundly defeated in a war with the new rising power in the Far East, Japan. One consequence of the defeat was Beijing's need for financial as well as diplomatic and military assistance. Once again, Russia took advantage of the situation and in exchange for a loan of 400,000,000 francs, backed by France, at an interest rate lower than those offered by Germany and Great Britain, extracted an agreement on May 22, 1896 to build the section of the Trans-Siberian Railway between Chita and Vladivostok across Manchuria—the Chinese Eastern

Railway.[5] This not only shortened the route by some 340 miles but also avoided some very difficult terrain that would have had to be traversed if the line were built only on Russian territory.

The agreement itself, the Li-Loban Treaty, was a mutual security pact that was to come into effect in case of an "aggression directed by Japan, whether against Russian territory in Eastern Asia, or against the territory of China or that of Korea." It further provided: "In order to facilitate the access of the Russian land troops to the menaced points, and to insure their means of subsistence, the Chinese government consents to the construction of a railway line across the Chinese provinces of Amur (i.e., the Heilungkiang) and of Guirin (Kirin) in the direction of Vladivostok. *The junction of this railway with the Russian railway shall not serve as a pretext for any encroachment on Chinese territory nor for any infringement of the rights of sovereignty of his Majesty the Emperor of China.*"[6]

Needless to point out, this last provision was egregiously violated by the Russians. Capitalizing further on China's lack of an effective bargaining position, Russia successfully pressured China into granting yet another concession in Manchuria on March 27, 1898, by which the Russians obtained both leases on the ports of Talien (Dairen) and Port Arthur on the Liaotung Peninsula and permission to build a major spur off the Chinese Eastern Railway connecting these ports with Harbin. Once again, the lease stated, "Consent to the construction of the railway on the basis indicated shall never under any form serve as a pretext for the seizure of Chinese territory or for an encroachment of the sovereign rights of China."[7]

Notwithstanding the solemnity with which such agreements were signed, Russia's intentions clearly were to ignore these commitments whenever it suited its purposes. This is evident from the July 1903 report of the Russian statesman Sergei I. Witte on the situation in the Far East. In his view the problem facing the European powers in the Far East was

to obtain as large a share as possible of the outlived Oriental states, especially of the Chinese Colossus. Russia, both geographically and historically, has the undisputed right to the lion's share of the expected prey. The elemental movement of the people eastward began under Ivan the Terrible. Continuing ever since, it has lately stopped with the occupation of the Kwantung Peninsula. Obviously, neither this territory nor Manchuria can be Russia's final goal. Given our enormous frontier line with China and our exceptionally favorable situation, the absorption by Russia of a considerable portion of the Chinese Empire is only a question of time, unless China succeeds in protecting itself. But our chief aim is to see that this absorption shall take place naturally, without seizing territory, in order to avoid a premature division of China by the Powers concerned, which would deprive Russia of China's most desirable province.[8]

By disregarding the conditional clauses of both the 1896 treaty and the 1898 lease, the Russians were now positioned to exercise hegemony over northern and central Manchuria. The general turbulence that resulted from the Boxer Rebellion (1899–1900) provided an appropriate justification for a Russian invasion of Manchuria. In his memoirs, Count Witte recorded the conversation he had at the time with the war minister, General Kuropatkin. "He was beaming with joy. I called his attention to the fact that the insurrection was the result of our seizure of the Kwantung [Liaotung] Peninsula. 'On my part,' he replied, 'I am very glad. This will give us an excuse for seizing Manchuria.' "[9]

Between July and September 1900 the Russians occupied all the strategic positions in the region from Heilongjiang to Fengt'ien. The Russians clearly intended to remain in Manchuria even after the withdrawal of the allies from Beijing. To provide legitimacy for this illegal occupation, they tried to force the Chinese into agreeing to a new treaty that would convert all of Manchuria into a Russian protectorate. This barely disguised attempt to seize Manchuria aroused strong opposition both among the Chinese and the rival foreign powers, particularly Japan. After intensive negotiations a Sino-Russian agreement was finally concluded on March 26, 1902, which called for the complete withdrawal of the Russians in three stages within 18 months. In April 1903, when the second stage of withdrawal was due, the Russians not only reneged on their promise but dispatched more troops into Manchuria and reoccupied Mukden.[10] Russian aims were blocked, however, by a confrontation with Japan, which viewed the Russian march across Manchuria as conflicting with its own imperial ambitions in the region.

Japan had earlier been disturbed by Russian moves toward Korea, a country the Japanese considered to be within their own sphere of interest. A Russo-Korean treaty of friendship had been signed in 1884, and, in the following year, the Russians tried to obtain control of Port Lazareff on the Korean coast through a secret arrangement. Implementation of this agreement was blocked by strong British opposition to it. In 1888, as Korea was beginning to emerge from its vassalage to China, another secret agreement was negotiated that effectively made Korea a Russian protectorate.

The Russian position in Korea was soon to be tested as a consequence of the war that broke out between China and Japan in 1894, which led to the Japanese invasion of Korea. This posed a strategic threat to the Russian Maritime Province and Vladivostok. Russia's actions in the face of this challenge are noteworthy. Recognizing the reality of the emerging power of Japan, Russia apparently was content to allow Korea nominally to come within the Japanese sphere of influence, at least for the time being. On the other hand, the demonstration of Japanese power caused Russia to join together with France and Germany to force Japan to withdraw from Manchuria. As compensation, Japan was to receive from China a large cash indemnity, which, as was discussed earlier, was loaned by Russia to advance its own position in Manchuria. Then, in February 1896, Russian forces occupied Seoul, evoking strong protests from Japan. This soon led to the Lobanov-Yamagata Treaty, which gave Russia the dominant interest in Korea's finances, whereas Japan's sphere of interest was limited to trade and industry. The aggressive implementation of the agreement by the Russians soon led to encroachment on Japan's sphere of interest, the former having contrived to have a Russian appointed as controller of Korean customs. Japanese protests led, in 1898, to the Rosen-Nishii Agreement, by which Russia promised to stay out of Korean trade matters and both nations agreed to keep out of Korean politics. Japan had been outfoxed by Russia and could do little but harbor its resentment for the time being.

War between the two states soon erupted over the Russian attempt to gain concessions along the Yalu River in northern Korea. A group of Russian speculators had organized the East Asiatic Company for Exploitation of Timber in Korea and Manchuria, and they persuaded Nicholas II to approve their proposal to exploit the timber resources along the Yalu. Lumbering operations began on the Korean side of the river in January 1904. Once again the Japanese protested vehemently, but to no avail. Negotiations to resolve the crisis broke down, and Japan broke diplomatic relations on February 6, 1904. Two days later the Russo-Japanese War broke out with a Japanese attack on Port Arthur, followed by a formal declaration of war on February 10. Notwithstanding its mutual security pact of 1896 with Russia, China stayed out of the war, which, on land, was fought in Manchuria.

The Russians were able to field about 80,000 troops that were already in place in the Far East, including railway guards and the garrisons at Vladivostok and Port Arthur. The Japanese had some 270,000 first-line troops that were thrown into the struggle. On the other hand, the Japanese had reserves of some 200,000 men, whereas the Russian reserves were practically unlimited. Notwithstanding the Russian general advantage in manpower, it could not be exploited effectively. The Russians had to transport their reserves across the length of Asia along the thin line of communication provided by the single-track Trans-Siberian Railway, at a maximum of 30,000 men a month.[11] Furthermore, the resupply of the Russian forces in the Far East required an extraordinary logistics operation that also relied almost exclusively on the use of the inadequate Trans-Siberian. In addition, as the Russian Baltic fleet moved to reinforce the Pacific flotilla, it was calculated that these ships would burn about 3,000 tons of coal a day. But unlike the British, the Russians had no chain of bases along the extended route around Africa and the China seas. The ability of the fleet to function out of range of its home coaling ports was dependent on a German firm that had promised to send colliers to rendezvous with the Russian fleet on the high seas.[12]

Once again the Russians learned the folly of committing themselves to distant operations without adequate lines of communication and forward supply bases. Another lesson of the war was the high risk of attempting to pass through the bottleneck of the Tsushima Strait during a period of hostilities with Japan. On May 27, 1905 the Russian fleet was caught and engaged off Tsushima by the Japanese navy and lost 32 of 36 vessels, which included 12 capital ships. Within a few days of this disaster, Czar Nicholas II accepted President Theodore Roosevelt's offer to mediate the conflict, which was brought to an end soon thereafter.

The Japanese were the undisputed victors in the Russo-Japanese War of 1904–5 and effectively blocked any further Russian advance in the region. Under the terms of the Treaty of Portsmouth (September 15, 1905), Russia turned over to Japan the South Manchurian Railway from Changchun to Port Arthur as well as their lease on that port. In addition, Japan received title to the southern half of Sakhalin Island (below 50 degrees north latitude). Both nations were to withdraw from Manchuria.

In 1911, however, taking advantage of the turmoil accompanying the overthrow of the Chinese monarchy, Russia advanced into Manchuria about 5 miles along a 60-mile stretch (some 375 square miles) in the Manchouli region between Mongolia and the Argun River. The Russians claimed that this territory was ceded under the Treaty of Tsisihar by local authorities who had seceded from China. Subsequent Chinese governments have refused to accept the legitimacy of this land grab.

Russia and Japan agreed in 1907 on the establishment of separate spheres of influence in China. Southern Manchuria and Inner Mongolia were to come within the Japanese sphere and northern Manchuria, Outer Mongolia, and Xinjiang were to be reserved for the Russians. As a consequence of this arrangement, the Russian sphere included virtually all of the territory north of what later came to be called the Kuropatkin Line. Named after General Kuropatkin, this was the line drawn by the imperial strategists in Saint Petersburg as a possible boundary between Russia and China in Asia. The Kuropatkin Line followed the forty-third parallel and stretched eastward from the Khan-Tengri range in the Tien-Shan to Vladivostok.[13]

At the turn of the century, the Chinese, frustrated by their apparent inability to hold their empire together, adopted a policy of seeking to dominate their outlying regions through sinicizing the population. Beijing encouraged Chinese peasant migrations into Outer Mongolia as part of a systematic colonization effort. In 1908 the Chinese garrison in the Mongolian capital, Urga, was reinforced, and intensive colonization began along the Kalgan-Urga caravan route through the Gobi Desert. In 1911 a Chinese bureau was opened in Urga to facilitate the colonization drive. It was not long before the Russians reacted to the implicit challenge of these events.

In July 1911, conveniently for Russian purposes, an anti-Chinese meeting was held in Urga that resulted in a petition to the czar imploring his help and protection against the growing Chinese suppression of the Mongolian people. The apparently Russian-instigated petition was addressed to "the omnipotent white Tsar of the great Russian people . . . [who] protects the yellow peoples and is himself the incarnation of virtue." It went on to suggest: "If we assist one another, we will not lose our former position. The yellow peoples will reign."[14] The implicit presumption that the Russians had an interest in establishing and preserving the self-rule of the Mongols appears almost absurd when one takes note that only a year earlier General Kuropatkin stated: "The 'Yellow Peril' can be checked, for a long time to come, by a uniform recognition of the fact that the preservation of peace in Asia is an all-European problem and by the readiness of all nations of Europe to unite their forces for the protection and strengthening of the position they now occupy in Asia. . . . In general, it would be an alliance of the White race against the peoples of the Yellow and Black races."[15]

In any case, the petition fulfilled its purpose as a pretext for Russian involvement. As was concluded at a conference on foreign affairs held in Saint Petersburg in 1911:

The reforms planned by China in Mongolia—Chinese tillers to colonize the strips of land bordering us, the linking of the same by railways, at points which would be close to this frontier, with Chinese administrative centers and the distribution of Chinese troops, especially the appearance of considerable Chinese armed forces in the close neighborhood of our possessions, cannot fail to disturb us. Therefore, the Mongolian question is for us of great importance, and our support of the Mongols in their aspiration to counteract the above-mentioned undertaking of the Chinese government would fully correspond with our interests.[16]

The Russians responded to the Mongol request with arms and other assistance, setting the stage for the direct intervention that was soon to follow.

Mongolia declared its independence almost immediately following the overthrow of the Chinese monarchy on October 11, 1911. On December 28 of that year, in a ceremony organized by the Russians, the Urga Living Buddha was designated as the Bogdo Khan, the secular ruler of Mongolia. In Inner Mongolia and among the Barguts of northwestern Manchuria, nationalist elements began clamoring for a political union with Outer Mongolia that would consolidate the Mongol peoples around the new independent Mongol state. However, an independent and possibly strong Mongolia in a region where they harbored expansionist ambitions was not what the Russians had in mind. They wanted Mongolia to serve as a weak buffer zone between themselves and the Chinese. Consequently, the Russians now acted to prevent the emergence of a strong Mongol state. They moved expeditiously to detach Mongolia's northwestern province of Urianghay, formally declaring it to be a Russian protectorate three years later. They then intervened directly in 1913 to force the new Mongolian government to acknowledge

Chinese suzerainty. The Kiakhta Agreement of June 7, 1915 subsequently reduced Mongolia from an independent state to an autonomous province within the Chinese empire, with Russia having extensive trade privileges there. In this manner, notwithstanding Chinese suzerainty, Mongolia became a de facto Russian protectorate. As observed by G. M. Friters, "by manoeuvering in such a manner as to prevent coalition between Chinese and Mongols, Russia was able to rule Mongolia by pretending that the Mongols were free, and also to keep the rest of the world from interfering with its monopoly, by allowing it to be inferred that the Mongols were not free."[17]

Emboldened by the overthrow of the czarist regime in 1917, China challenged the autonomous status of Outer Mongolia and sent its troops into the region in 1919, under the pro-Japanese General Hsiu Chouchen. This created the impression among some observers that the Chinese intervention was also serving Japanese interests. It was interpreted by some as a Japanese-sponsored maneuver to replace Russian control of Outer Mongolia with an indirect Japanese control exercised through Chinese agents.[18] Hsiu reached Urga in October 1919, and in the following month the Mongols dutifully requested the abrogation of their autonomy. Chinese troops remained in the Mongolian capital until February 1921, when the city fell to a force of Mongols and "White" Russians under Baron Ungern-Sternberg.

On March 1, 1921 the Soviets helped organize the Mongolian People's Revolutionary party, which held its first congress in the Soviet Union at Kiakhta, near the Mongolian border. On March 13 it formed the Provisional People's Revolutionary Government of Mongolia, which on April 10 petitioned the Soviet Union for assistance in warding off the counterrevolutionary forces that were conducting a reign of terror in the country. In response to this request, Soviet troops then entered Mongolia and occupied Urga (soon to be renamed Ulan Bator) in July over the protests of China. On November 5, 1921 the Mongolian communist government signed a treaty with the Soviet Union and requested that Soviet troops not be withdrawn until the region was completely secure. The Soviet response was framed in a manner that is remarkably contemporary. "Having firmly decided to withdraw its troops from the territory of autonomous Mongolia, which is bound to Soviet Russia only by the ties of mutual friendship and common interests, just as soon as the menace to the free development of the Mongolian people and to the security of the Russian Republic and the Far Eastern Republic shall have been removed, the Russian government of Mongolia notes that this moment has not yet arrived.''[19]

At the same time the Soviet government reasserted Russian authority over Urianghay, which in 1921 declared itself the independent republic of Tannu-Tuva and became incorporated into the RSFSR as the Tuvinian Autonomous Oblast on October 13, 1944. Tannu-Tuva is a strategically located territory that is of considerable geopolitical significance in Inner Asia. From a security standpoint, Soviet control of Tannu-Tuva makes the southern borders of Siberia largely impregnable to ground attack from forces approaching through Xinjiang.[20] From a geostrategic perspective, as Peter S. H. Tang points out, ''with Tannu Tuva lost to Russia, China or an independent Outer Mongolia would be left in a very strategically disadvantageous position: what was formerly a spearhead of northern defense would become a foreign-controlled natural stronghold which would point to the heart of Western Mongolia and its center, Uliassutai, endangering the security of Sinkiang Province.''[21]

However, the Soviets were unwilling to allow the question of Outer Mongolia to interfere with the normalization of relations with China. Thus, notwithstanding their earlier commitments to the Mongols, in the Treaty of Peking (May 31, 1924) the Soviets recognized nominal Chinese sovereignty over the region, though they themselves retained actual control by means of their influence with the political leadership, which had eliminated any residual anti-Soviet elements in a coup that took place on August 30. With the death of the Living Buddha a month earlier, Outer Mongolia became the Mongolian People's Republic. Notwithstanding Moscow's undertakings in the Treaty of Peking, as Chicherin, the Soviet commissar for foreign affairs, made abundantly clear toward the end of the year, no attempt by China to assert its sovereignty in Outer Mongolia would be acceptable or permitted by the Soviet Union. In a formulation that left the notion of formal Chinese sovereignty without any substantive content, he declared, ''We recognize the Mongolian People's Republic as part of the Chinese Republic, but we recognize also its autonomy in so far-reaching a sense that we regard it not only as independent of China in its internal affairs, but also as capable of pursuing its foreign policy independently.''[22]

The threat to Mongolia from China receded into the background in face of the new threat emerging from the Japanese takeover of Manchuria and its transformation into the puppet state of Manchukuo. This precipitated the Soviet-Mongolian ''gentlemen's agreement'' of November 27, 1934, which brought Soviet troops (withdrawn in 1925) back into the country shortly thereafter. Because of continuing Japanese pressure on the frontier, Stalin announced on March 1, 1936 that the Soviet Union would defend Mongolia. On March 12, Moscow and Ulan Bator signed an agreement that amounted to a de facto defense alliance.[23]

Imperial Russia also had designs on the large western province of Xinjiang, where Chinese control had long been tenuous at best. The province was effectively split in two by the Tien-shan range, which served as an effective barrier between Dzhungaria to the north and Kashgaria to the south. Russia apparently had seriously considered the idea of annexing Dzhungaria, thereby extending its central Siberian frontier south as far as the Tien-shan. Though Russia might have preferred to take all of Xinjiang, the Tarim Basin in Kashgaria was too close to India, and any attempt at annexation might have precipitated a conflict with Great Britain.[24] Nonetheless, as was discussed by E. V. G. Kiernan in his history of the diplomacy of the era: "the interests of Russia and England in Eastern Turkestan [Xinjiang] were real, intensive and intimately connected with the broader policies being pursued throughout the continent. As in Afghanistan, their interests collided there and the conflict was resolved only after a long diplomatic duel. It was the possible strategic danger that led to the idea of adding Kashgar to the buffer-states of the Indian Empire and so to the British recognition of Yakub Beg in 1874."[25]

Concerned about the threat of a collision with Britain that could precipitate the latter's advance north beyond the bounds of India, which would place it astride Russian Central Asia, Saint Petersburg chose the course of prudence and decided to allow Xinjiang to remain a buffer between the two empires.

After the revolution in China, and more especially after the revolution in Russia, Xinjiang became a virtually self-governing unit within a Soviet sphere of influence, and it remained under the effective control of the Soviet army until the army was withdrawn after the outbreak of war between Germany and the Soviet Union. The Soviet interest remained primarily economic, and by 1934, Moscow controlled virtually all the trade of the region. Nonetheless, the pervasive Soviet presence in the province led to charges by Japan regarding the "Sovietization of Sinkiang." On January 28, 1935, Molotov, in a speech to the Seventh All-Union Congress of Soviets, responded to the Japanese statement as follows: "It remains for me to say a few words on the slanderous rumours about the Sovietization of Sinkiang. . . . I consider it necessary to emphasize the real Soviet policy towards China: the Soviet Union considers as incompatible with its policy the seizure of foreign territories, and is an absolute adherent of the independence, integrity, and sovereignty of China over all her parts including Sinkiang."[26]

With the civil war in China creating increasing chaos to the east, the Soviets were once again content to leave the province as a buffer zone against any spillover of the conflict into Asiatic Russia.

The Russian imperialist expansion across Asia was thus accomplished in large measure at the expense of China. Though the Ch'ing emperors had been overlords of Manchuria, Inner and Outer Mongolia, Tibet, and a good part of Turkestan in Central Asia, their actual control of these lands was tenuous. The border regions tended to be, and remain today, populated by largely non–ethnic Chinese peoples. The Russians took full advantage of the weaknesses of the loosely strung Chinese empire, applying pressures that led in the mid nineteenth century to the imposition of a pattern of treaties and agreements that ostensibly legitimated Russia's seizure of territories in Inner Asia, the Mongolian plateau, and the Far East. One of the major factors that contributed to the aggressive policies of the Russians, in addition to the imperial tradition of expansion, was the relative insecurity of their critical lines of communication across Asia, which was itself a direct consequence of their expansionism. Having built the Trans-Siberian Railway to facilitate their control of the vast territory, they now had to expand to ensure the security of the railroad, particularly where it passed close to the Chinese and Mongolian borders. The Russian imperialists, followed by their Soviet heirs, thus entrapped themselves in this seemingly endless pattern of expansion followed by a need for further expansion to secure the fruits of the earlier expansion.

Notes

1. O. Edmund Clubb, *China and Russia: The "Great Game,"* p. 9.
2. For the text of the treaty, see Basil Dmytryshyn, ed., *Russia's Conquest of Siberia 1558–1700*, vol. 1, pp. 497–500.
3. Cited by Tien-fang Cheng, in William G. Bray, *Russian Frontiers: From Muscovy to Khrushchev*, pp. 51–52.

4. Bray, op. cit., p. 52.
5. George Vernadsky, *A History of Russia*, p. 179.
6. Cited by Bray, op. cit., p. 58 (emphasis Bray's).
7. Ibid., p. 60.
8. Sergei I. Witte, *The Memoirs of Count Witte*, pp. 121–22.
9. Ibid., pp. 107–8.
10. Robert H. G. Lee, *The Manchurian Frontier in Ch'ing History*, p. 138.
11. O. Edmund Clubb, *Twentieth Century China*, p. 31.
12. David Fairhall, *Russia Looks to the Sea*, p. 22.
13. W. A. Douglas Jackson, *The Russo-Chinese Borderlands*, p. 53.
14. Cited by Tien-fong Cheng, in Bray, op. cit., p. 54.
15. Cited by Bray, op. cit., pp. 54–5.
16. Cited by Peter S. H. Tang, *Russian and Soviet Policy in Manchuria and Outer Mongolia, 1911–1931*, p. 297.
17. G. M. Friters, "The Prelude to Outer Mongolian Independence," *Pacific Affairs*, June 1937, p. 189.
18. G. M. Friters, "The Development of Outer Mongolian Independence," *Pacific Affairs*, September 1937, p. 315.
19. Cited by Tien-fong Cheng, in Bray, op. cit., p. 56.
20. Fedor S. Mansvetov, "Russia and China in Outer Mongolia," *Foreign Affairs*, October 1945, p. 148.
21. Tang, op. cit., p. 400.
22. Ibid., p. 382.
23. Max Beloff, *The Foreign Policy of Soviet Russia*, vol. 1, pp. 246–47.
24. Louis Fischer, *The Soviets in World Affairs*, vol. 2, p. 534.
25. E. V. G. Kiernan, *British Diplomacy in China, 1880–1885*, p. 38.
26. Cited by Beloff, op. cit., pp. 237–38.

6   *The Current Geostrategic Posture*

The post–World War II expansion of the Soviet *imperium* to its present configuration has been witnessed and accepted by the free world with remarkable complacency. Notwithstanding some occasionally fiery rhetoric about containing Soviet expansionism, the West has for the most part been immobilized in the face of an unrelenting drive by Moscow for global hegemony. It was widely believed, and indeed continues to be the fervent hope of many despite all the evidence to the contrary, that the risks of escalation to nuclear war would serve as a deterrent to Soviet adventurism. That this is a fanciful notion should become painfully obvious if one simply tallies the lands from Eastern Europe to Asia, Africa, and Latin America that have been added to the *imperium* between 1945, when the United States had a total nuclear monopoly, and the present, with its uncertain nuclear balance of power. It is surely true that the dangers of escalation to nuclear war have caused the Soviets to be particularly circumspect in avoiding head-on collisions with the West. However, it is equally true that the responses of the West to Soviet adventures have been similarly circumspect. Thus, as a practical matter, tactics aside, the threat of nuclear confrontation has had little impact on Soviet empire building in the second half of the twentieth century. With hardly anyone in a position of political authority and responsibility in the West prepared seriously to pursue a program of actively rolling back Soviet advances, the residual hope seems to be that somehow the Soviet system will collapse of its own accord, leading its empire simply to disintegrate, as it began to do after the Russian Revolution, the expectation being that, as the economic, social, political, and strategic pressures on Moscow intensify, in the words of Milan Hauner, "it might become a herculean task to contain them all without a fundamental reorganization of the Soviet Eurasian empire which, after all, is an anachronistic survivor of the age of imperial expansion and colonization."[1]

The Soviet Union, as an imperial conglomerate, is indeed plagued by numerous and increasingly worrisome political, economic, and strategic dilemmas that threaten to unravel the achievement of centuries of empire building. Moscow must cope with the problems generated by the revolution in communications that has effectively destroyed its ability to insulate its far-flung borders from the penetration of influences from the world outside. It is no longer generally feasible for the Kremlin to make a credible case for denying the natural desire of its peoples for a freer and better life on the basis of a continuing threat of "capitalist encirclement" that seeks to destroy the achievements of socialism. Saddled with a relatively stagnant and inefficient economy, Moscow is confronted by the dilemma of how to bring about economic reform in a manner that does not undermine the elaborate structure of state control upon which the entire Soviet edifice is based. This problem is compounded by that of how far to allow its satellite and client states to make these same changes, which may engender serious geopolitical consequences for the integrity of Moscow's control of its empire. Finally, the Kremlin is confronted by the recognition that, if the Soviet *imperium* does not continue to expand, it may well begin to contract. For the empire is not an integral whole but is made up of discrete components many of which would prefer independence if such an option were attainable. And the Soviet leaders know quite well that empires that do not continue to grow soon begin to stagnate and come apart, starting at the more exposed extremities, which are the most difficult to control. Thus, though it could be argued that the economic and political incentives for Soviet expansion are greater today than at any time in Russian history—never before did the Russian ruling regime *require* imperial expansion as a condition of its survival—the Soviet Union is confronted by a number of serious geostrategic dilemmas on its western, southern, and eastern flanks that constrain Moscow's options.

For the Soviet Union, the factors of geography and demography that facilitated the formation of an empire stretching for almost half the circumference of the globe, from East Germany to North Korea, are the very same considerations that could facilitate the contraction of that empire to its sixteenth-century dimensions. The contemporary national security policies of the Soviet Union and the geostrategic underpinnings of its foreign policy are conditioned by these factors, perhaps the foremost of which concern the stability and defensibility of the imperial frontiers.

The harsh topographical reality is that, between Moscow and the Atlantic Ocean across Central Europe, there are no natural barriers that could provide the basis for a defensive sealing of the Soviet imperial frontier. In the absence of any significant natural barriers, what separates the Soviet empire from the free states of Western Europe is the political-military boundary drawn between NATO and the Moscow-dominated Warsaw Pact. Moscow is well aware, however, that the Warsaw Pact nations serve more as buffers between the Soviet Union and Western Europe than as participants in a viable defensive alliance of communist states. Indeed, from a strategic perspective, it may be argued that the primary value of the Warsaw Pact states is in securing the lines of communication between the Soviet Union and its forward positions in East Germany.

Though Soviet operational doctrine calls for coalition warfare, which is predicated on the active involvement of the armed forces of the pact members to bolster Soviet capabilities, the doctrine assumes that ''Soviet military forces must play the primary role in all military operations, with no primary military task entrusted to any East European army on its own. East European units cannot replace Soviet military units.''[2] When conceived, this doctrine faithfully reflected the preeminent position of Central Europe in Soviet geopolitical priorities. In the 1980s, however, that priority has been eroded as the requirement for the deployment of Soviet military capability elsewhere, particularly in Asia, increases. Thus, at a time when Soviet dependence on the Eastern European states to carry their share of the military burden in Central Europe is increasing, Moscow is also confronted by the increasingly probable prospect of nonperformance at a time of crisis by one or more of the armies of its Eastern European allies. The potential reliability of the Warsaw Pact armies would be questionable even in the unlikely event of a NATO attack on Eastern Europe. Where it was not a matter of defending their own homelands but simply of serving as the instruments of Soviet ambitions in Western Europe, the incentives for compliance with Moscow's wishes begin to diminish rapidly. This presents the Kremlin with a serious strategic dilemma.

It has been noted by many analysts that, as formidable as their forces have come to be, the Soviets would have great difficulty in launching and sustaining a major attack on the West without active backing by their allies. While Moscow might well be able to amass the required numbers of Soviet men and equipment for an attack on the critical central region of Europe, this would necessitate a major preliminary redeployment of forces from the Soviet Union, a move that would cost it the critical element of surprise.[3] Furthermore, many of these same forces, including some 30 divisions currently deployed behind the Soviet border in Eastern Europe, are required to ensure internal security in the satellite countries. The likelihood of their being needed for this purpose would most likely increase significantly were a war to break out with the West. The mustering of the needed troop strength would then probably necessitate the withdrawal of the required forces from Asia, leaving China free to resolve unilaterally its various territorial claims against the Soviet Union, as well as to endanger the very viability of the Soviet state in Asia.

Soviet strategy for securing its western flank in Europe thus consists of two fundamental elements. First, Moscow must continue to maintain effective control of East Germany, Poland, Czechoslovakia, and Hungary, which provide it both with the strategic depth necessary to consolidate its position for defense and with the forward positions for effective power projection. Second, Moscow must find means for undermining the strength and viability of the Western alliance. Since NATO is a maritime alliance, its strategic depth lies in its control of the seas. Colin Gray has observed: "A continental landpower cannot be defeated at sea, but a maritime alliance most certainly can be. A seapower such as the United States must command the sea lines of communication to peripheral Eurasia, both to sustain combat on land and to develop, and threaten to develop, new axes of assault upon the geographically very extended fortress of the heartland power."[4]

Since a conflict between NATO and the Warsaw Pact must inevitably be decided on land, the ability of NATO to prevail becomes almost entirely contingent on its success in maintaining control of the lines of communications between Western Europe and the United States. Were the U.S. and allied navies to be defeated, the conflict would just as inevitably be decided against the West. As was pointed out by Seth Cropsey, "more than 90 percent of all the material needed to fight a land war in Europe would have to go by sea; a single mechanized division requires more than 1,000 tons delivered each day to sustain operations. Unless the United States and its allies can secure the seas, we cannot survive on land.[5]

Accordingly, the successful extension of Moscow's reach into Western Europe requires that Soviet forces be positioned both to interdict the flow of NATO reinforcements and war material from the United States and Canada and to successfully engage those NATO forces committed to the defense of the sea lanes. At a minimum, the Soviet northern fleet based at the Kola Peninsula must have unimpeded access to the North Atlantic in order to interrupt the NATO supply lines. However, even this minimum requirement cannot be fulfilled satisfactorily as long as Norway remains committed to NATO and prepared to help control access to the open seas along its extensive coastline. In the view of some analysts, even Soviet control of all of Norway would not ensure free access to the Atlantic by their submarines and aircraft. To be assured of the ability to contest NATO's lines of communication in the North Atlantic, the Soviets might first have to seize Iceland, and perhaps even part of Greenland. Milan Vego argues that "whoever controls Iceland holds the keys to the Northern Atlantic. . . . Iceland flanks the 1,530-nm route which the Soviet submarines and aircraft must pass through to reach the open waters of the Atlantic."[6]

Nevertheless, were the Soviets able to seize control of Norway and the surrounding seas, they not only would have gained a forward position relative to the critical NATO sea lines of communication, but they would also be poised to outflank Denmark and the Low Countries, thereby bringing about the collapse of the entire northern flank. Short of such a direct assault, the Soviets might still be able to achieve relatively unhindered access to the Atlantic sea lanes through the political neutralization of Norway, a goal that they are currently pursuing vigorously.

To the south, from the Black Sea to India, Moscow faces a region of endemic instability that leaves its southern flank uncomfortably exposed. It is only here in the Middle East, except for the Russo-Finnish and Russo-Norwegian borders, that the Soviet Union comes into direct physical contact with the noncommunist world.[7] Some analysts consider the region to have become one of prime importance for the Soviets because of the possible deployment of U.S. nuclear missile submarines in the northwest quadrant of the Indian Ocean. Such a deployment would constitute a potential threat to all major Soviet industrial centers between the Ukraine and eastern Siberia.[8] This would place a heavy burden on the Soviets to be able to gain some measure of control in the region in order to offset U.S. naval power projection capabilities. It would also require substantial antisubmarine warfare capabilities in an area where the Soviets had no ports or forward bases.

Since January 1968, when Russia's long-standing nemesis in Asia, Great Britain, announced its intention to withdraw from the region "east of Suez," the Indian Ocean basin has constituted a power vacuum that the Soviet Union is attempting to fill. Moscow's immediate concern was to prevent the replacement of British power and influence by that of the United States. Thus, when Iran's Prime Minister Hoveida publicly opposed any attempt by a nonregional power to assume Britain's historic role as regional peacekeeper, Moscow was quick to lend its full support to Iran. *Tass* stated on March 3, 1968:

The Soviet Union, loyal to its policy of protecting the national interests of sovereign countries and peoples against the encroachments of imperialists, and realizing that these plans of neocolonialism are directed against the security of the southern frontiers of the USSR as well, comes out resolutely against the new attempts by aggressive circles in the United States and Britain to interfere in the affairs of the countries in the area of the Persian Gulf and to dictate their will to those countries.

The peoples of those countries, and they alone, have the right to shape their destiny. The sooner an end is put to colonialism and neocolonialism in that area, the more successfully will the task of transforming the Middle East into a zone of lasting peace and international cooperation be accomplished.

The following year, the United States promulgated the Nixon Doctrine, which placed the major responsibility for regional peacekeeping on the states of the area, meaning, in effect, pro-Western Iran under the shah. With the overthrow of the Pahlevi regime a decade later, followed by the outbreak of the Iraq-Iran War and the Soviet intervention in Afghanistan, the region has become engulfed by a number of raging conflicts, insurrections, and intrigues, which have engendered further instability.

The collapse of the shah's regime also spelled the end of the Nixon Doctrine. In its place, a decade later, came the Carter Doctrine, which declared the region under discussion, particularly that of the Persian Gulf and Arabian Sea, to be of vital interest to the United States. To be in a position to defend its security interests in the area, the United States began a limited buildup of naval-based power that can be projected ashore if necessary. At present, this capability resides primarily in the Indian Ocean island of Diego Garcia, where the Rapid Deployment Force maintains 17 military container ships loaded with sufficient tanks, armored personnel carriers, rocket launchers, and other equipment to sustain a force of 12,500 marines in combat without resupply for 30 days.[9] While these forces are quite modest compared to Soviet strength in Afghanistan and in nearby Soviet Central Asia, they nonetheless pose a challenge to Moscow's goal of achieving undisputed control over the region.

However, the Soviets' main concern is with the substantial U.S. naval presence, and they have been conducting a long-term propaganda campaign to try to force the withdrawal of U.S. naval forces from the region. As part of this effort, the Soviet Union has become an ardent rhetorical advocate of converting the Indian Ocean into a "zone of peace," at least until it is itself fully capable of filling the regional power vacuum.

From Moscow eastward across and around the low and easily penetrable Urals, there lies the vast Eurasian plain, which stretches as far as Mongolia. Because of the absence of any major natural barriers, this plain has served as the route of successive waves of migrations, as well as invading armies, which have moved across it for centuries. As remarked by John J. Stephan, the very "awareness of the plain's historic permeability and ethnic evanescence leaves many Russians with a half-formed sense of territorial insecurity that manifests itself not only in the predilection for strong central authority but in what amounts to a national fixation on frontier defense."[10]

On its eastern frontiers, the Soviet Union faces an enigmatic China, with which it shares a common border stretching for thousands of miles from Central Asia to the Pacific Ocean. China, because of its size and enormous population, poses a dilemma for Soviet strategy and policy that defies simple solution. Its geostrategic position impedes Moscow's ability to project power southward to the periphery of East Asia and bars a direct land route from the Soviet Union to its major Southeast

Asian ally, Vietnam. Furthermore, China has made clear its intention to pursue an independent foreign policy, one major element of which is a blossoming military supply and technology transfer relationship with the United States. At a minimum, Moscow must seek to prevent this relationship from emerging into a de facto defense alliance between China and the United States. The most that the Soviets might reasonably hope for in the foreseeable future would be an understanding between the two countries that would amount to a condominium in Asia, with China committing itself to remain neutral with respect to any potential Soviet-U.S. confrontation in the Asia-Pacific theater. The unrelenting Chinese hostility to the Soviet position in Asia over the past two decades has proven extremely nettlesome to Moscow. Given the tenuousness of the Soviet relationship with China, and the uncertainty regarding Chinese aims and ambitions in Asia, Moscow must once again face the disconcerting prospect of a two-front conflict at opposite ends of the Eurasian land mass.

The Problem of China

The communist takeover in China in 1949 portended a new era for the Sino-Soviet borderlands of Manchuria, Inner and Outer Mongolia, and Xinjiang. A new geopolitical environment seemed to have been created by the shared ideology between Moscow and Beijing, which suggested the emergence in the 1950s of a gigantic monolith spreading across Eurasia from East Berlin to Hanoi. There may have even been some hope in Moscow that China might ultimately become a Soviet satellite similar to those of Eastern Europe and thus serve as the vehicle for Soviet power projection to the western Pacific basin. However, in the early 1960s, after the Sino-Soviet dispute had developed into a virtual "cold war," it became evident that beneath the veneer of proletarian internationalism and communist fraternalism lurked the conflicting ambitions of Russian and Chinese nationalism.

It was then made public that as early as 1954, on the heels of the death of Stalin the previous year, Mao Zedong had approached the new Soviet leaders Khrushchev and Bulganin with regard to a proposed change in the existing political status of Outer Mongolia. Not surprisingly, they refused to consider opening any discussions on the question. That same year, *A Short History of Modern China* was published in Beijing. The book contained an illustration that showed Outer Mongolia as an integral part of China, and it outlined those territories that had been detached from China more than a century earlier, including the Soviet Far East, the Pamirs, and other regions along the Sino-Soviet frontiers.

In March 1963, in an article calculated to raise eyebrows in Moscow, the *People's Daily* publicly raised the issue of the losses of Chinese territory to Russian imperialism in the nineteenth century. It also indicated that China did not consider the status of any of these territories as beyond reconsideration and reversion.

In the hundred years or so prior to the victory of the Chinese revolution, the imperialist and colonial powers—the United States, Britain, France, Tsarist Russia, Germany, Japan, Italy, Austria, Belgium, the Netherlands, Spain and Portugal—carried out unbridled aggression against China. They compelled the governments of old China to sign a large number of unequal treaties: the Treaty of Nanking in 1842, the Treaty of Aigun in 1858, the Treaty of Tientsin in 1858, the Treaty of Peking in 1860, the Treaty of Ili of 1881, the Protocol of Lisbon of 1887, the Treaty of Shimonoseki of 1898, the Convention for the Extension of Hong Kong of 1898, the Treaty of 1901, etc. By virtue of these unequal treaties, they annexed Chinese territory in the north, south, east and west and held leased territories on the seaboard and in the hinterland of China . . .

At the time the People's Republic of China was inaugurated, our government declared that it would examine the treaties concluded by previous Chinese governments with foreign governments, treaties that had been left over by history, and would recognize, abrogate, revise or renegotiate them according to their respective contents.[11]

On September 3, 1963, Beijing accused Moscow of having carried out "large-scale subversive activities in the Ili region in Sinkiang," and on September 21, Moscow reciprocated with a verbal attack on the Chinese for systematically violating the Soviet frontier and attempting illegally to annex disputed territory at the confluence of the Ussuri and Amur Rivers.[12] Obviously upset by the emerging Chinese challenge to the legitimacy of Soviet borders in Asia, Moscow warned, "The artificial creation of any territorial problems in our times, especially between Socialist countries, would be tantamount to embarking on a very dangerous path."[13] Undeterred by mounting Soviet pique, in a remark calculated to upset the Soviets even further, Mao Zedong observed during an interview on July 10, 1964, "China has not yet asked the

Soviet Union for an accounting about Vladivostok, Khabarovsk, Kamchatka, and other towns and regions east of Lake Baikal which became Russian territory about 100 years ago."[14]

The Sino-Soviet border in the Far East is highly permeable. The Argun, Amur, and Ussuri rivers serve as natural boundaries for only half the year, since the rivers are frozen solid for the other half. Below the point where the Bureia and Amur rivers meet, there is a string of mountains on each side. On the Russian side, along the Ussuri, south of Khabarovsk, the terrain rises sharply to the coastal Sikhota-Alin range. But neither this nor the mountains about 100 miles to the north of the Amur offer much protection because the vast majority of the region's population, and nearly all its productive capacity, are crammed into the several river valleys. Consequently, as the recriminations between Beijing and Moscow escalated, deepening the growing Sino-Soviet rift, the Soviets began an incremental reinforcement of their military units along the frontier. With China becoming a nuclear power in 1964, followed by its construction of an intercontinental ballistic missile testing range in 1965, the Soviet Union began to see China as a potentially dangerous military threat.

By 1964, the year in which China joined the nuclear club, it was abundantly clear that any hopes of Chinese collusion in Soviet ambitions were vain illusions. If the Soviet Union were to become the dominant power in the Asia-Pacific theater and be able to exploit that position to realize significant strategic and political as well as economic benefits, it would have to find alternative means of establishing its power along the periphery of the continent. Moscow would have to make use of its own unfavorably situated maritime territories as the base for power projection. This would require not only an extensive military buildup in the Far East but also a major program of industrial development to provide an economic base for sustaining independently a large military infrastructure in an underdeveloped and relatively remote part of the Soviet Union. As Z. Mieczowski has argued, "it is reasonable to conclude that the increased attention paid by the Soviets to the development of the region has limited importance from a purely economic point of view and is strongly associated with military and strategic concerns. Between hostile China to the south, and unfriendly North America to the east and north, the Soviet Far East gains in importance as a forward base of the USSR's military strength."[15]

In 1969 a serious border crisis developed that had long-lasting effects on Sino-Soviet relations. On March 2, Chinese forces ambushed and inflicted heavy casualties on a Soviet unit on Chenbao (known to the Soviets as Damansky), a frozen island in the Ussuri River between the Soviet Maritime Province and Manchuria. On March 15 a Soviet force retaliated in kind and overwhelmed a Chinese force on the same island. That same day, Moscow warned, "The Soviet government declares that if the legitimate rights of the U.S.S.R. are mocked, that if new attempts are made to violate the integrity of Soviet territory, the Soviet Union and all of its peoples will defend it resolutely and will oppose a crushing riposte to such violations."[16] This was followed on June 13 by a virtual ultimatum from Moscow demanding consultations with Beijing on the border problem within two to three months. On the date of the two-month deadline, August 13, Soviet forces occupied a hill two kilometers beyond the border on the Chinese side, in western Xinjiang, and they defied the Chinese to force them out. The crisis was defused several weeks later when border negotiations began on October 20, continuing periodically ever since without any resolution of any of the fundamental issues between the two countries. The most recent renewal of bilateral talks on the perennial border problem began in Moscow on February 9, 1987.

One of the unintended consequences for the Soviet Union of the 1969 Sino-Soviet flare-up was the reintroduction of a U.S. presence in mainland China for the first time since the Communist takeover 20 years earlier. Faced by the threat of war with the Soviet Union in the north at a time when U.S. forces were heavily engaged in Vietnam to its south, China was placed in the uncomfortble position of confronting the possibility of a two-front war with the two superpowers, an uninviting prospect at best. It was clear to Mao Zedong that if he had to choose between them in order to alleviate the simultaneous pressure on both flanks, it was in China's best interest to reach an accommodation with the United States. Accordingly, in 1969, China effectively closed its borders to both the overland and overflight shipment of supplies from the Soviet Union to North Vietnam. It is noteworthy that the Chinese began to impede Soviet rail shipments across China in January 1969, well before the border crisis erupted in March.[17] This signaled an unmistakable and premeditated overture to the United States and not merely an arbitrary reaction to immediate events in the north. It was but one of a series of initiatives that culminated in the establishment of friendly relations between the two countries and in an emerging military assistance relationship that is of obvious concern to Moscow.

In addition, the Soviets were directly penalized by the closure of their line of communications across China to Vietnam. They now had to supply their ally by ship at a time when the Suez Canal was closed. This necessitated the establishment of a maritime supply line stretching from Odessa to Haiphong around Africa, an experience reminiscent of the problems faced by the Russian fleet during the Russo-Japanese War. The Kremlin was acutely aware of just how vulnerable its southern sea route was to interdiction by U.S. naval forces, were Washington prepared to risk widening the conflict by interfering with the Soviet resupply of North Vietnam.

In the midst of the 1969 crisis in Sino-Soviet relations, Leonid Brezhnev proposed the establishment of an Asian collective security system with the initial membership to include India, Pakistan, Afghanistan, Burma, Singapore, and Cambodia.[18] The proposal, which was received with little interest by the independent states of Asia, seemed clearly aimed at China. Even though China was later offered the opportunity of becoming "a full member of this system,"[19] it would be at a time when it would have to join on terms already set by the Soviets. Needless to say, Beijing was vehemently opposed to what it saw quite clearly and correctly as an attempt by Moscow to establish a *cordon sanitaire* around China.

At the same time, Moscow began to reinforce further its conventional and nuclear forces along the Chinese border and in the Mongolian People's Republic. By 1973, Soviet strength there reached some 50 divisions backed by substantial air power. Since then, the amount of Soviet power deployed along the long frontier has reached awesome proportions. Nonetheless, the Soviets continue to have much to worry about from China.

Of particular concern is the dramatic change in Chinese military doctrine and organization that began to take shape around 1980. Until then, Chinese doctrine was essentially defensive in character. Its growing nuclear force was to serve as a strategic deterrent, while its huge people's militia stood ready to conduct massive guerrilla war operations were China to be attacked by conventional forces. The new doctrine that emerged called for a strategic nuclear deterrent force combined with a three-million-man general-purpose and modernized conventional army for use in nonnuclear warfare situations. The question that the Soviets must grapple with is why China has elected to forgo its traditional people's army and build instead a large mechanized force with significant offensive capabilities.

One possible answer relates to the fact that the terrain characteristics of the vast territories of Inner Asia (running from the Amur basin in the northeast in a generally southwest direction for some 3,000 miles, straddling Mongolia and Xinjiang) lend themselves especially well to mechanized rather than positional warfare. These sparsely populated steppe and desert frontier regions, on both sides of the Sino-Soviet border, are particularly susceptible to encroachment.[20] Should demographic pressures in China precipitate a significant population movement in the direction of Soviet Central Asia, the need for a large modernized and mobile military force to clear the way becomes self-evident.

Soviet concerns over the security of the frontier in Inner Asia today would seem to echo those articulated by General A. N. Kuropatkin in a report to the czar on February 1, 1917. "As far as China is concerned, the future danger for Russia from this empire of 400,000,000 people is beyond all doubt. The most vulnerable part of the Russian frontier, as 800 years ago, remains that great gateway through which the hordes of Genghis Khan poured into Europe. . . . This gateway [Xinjiang] must not be left in the hands of the Chinese."[21]

Edgar O'Ballance has set out what he calls Gorbachev's "nightmare scenario," which depicts the character that a Chinese military aggression against the Soviet Union might take once China's force modernization program is completed. As an initial step, the Chinese would use their superior manpower to advantage and begin a widespread war of attrition, probably along the entire length of the Sino-Soviet frontier. This phase of the conflict would not be prosecuted from fixed positions. Instead, it would consist of numerous simultaneous probes in force. This would tend to stretch the smaller opposing Soviet forces thin, thereby enabling the Chinese to edge them back incrementally from the frontier.

Once having succeeded in forcing a significant thinning of Soviet forces along the length of the frontier, the Chinese would next proceed to sever their lines of communication and subject the now isolated frontier regions to ever tightening pincers. Gorbachev would then have to consider if the time was right to escalate the conflict to the nuclear level. However, he would have to make such a decision without any certainty that he could prevent a Chinese second strike that would result in millions of Soviet casualties and the destruction of some major cities. Furthermore, he would be running this enormous risk not to gain a decisive victory, but most probably "simply to gain a respite in a war he knows he could not ultimately win, as the odds are on the much more populous Chinese nation. A nuclear attack, even from the tiny Chinese arsenal, would cause death and destruction in the USSR on a sufficiently wide scale to make the price of a few square miles of Asian terrain far too pyrrhic. Gorbachev wakes up in a cold sweat from his nightmare scenario to realize that one day he may have to fight, and lose, a conventional war against China."[22]

Though the Chinese threat may be mitigated in the near term through negotiations leading to a temporary accommodation, the long-term strategic dilemma for the Soviet Union continues to fester.

Implacable Chinese hostility toward the Soviet Union for some two decades was reflected in an ongoing verbal onslaught that Moscow found disconcerting and embarrassing. As recently as September 1981, Vice Foreign Minister Zhang Wenjin stated at the United Nations: "It would be contrary to the international scene to consider that the Soviet Union is on the defensive and that its deep predicament is forcing it to consider a retreat. The facts in the past year have shown that the Soviet Union has not given up its bid for world hegemony, and the corollary strategy of a southward drive remains unchanged."[23]

Starting in 1982, however, the Chinese adopted a rather different tone with respect to the Soviet Union. There is good reason to believe that the change in Chinese attitude was closely related to the significant enhancement of U.S. military capability under the Reagan administration, which began to erode the Soviet margin of superiority in a number of areas. As a result, China could adopt a position of greater neutrality between the superpowers. Accordingly, as noted by Carol L. Hamrin, "trends in Chinese commentary after March implied, in contrast, that some acts of Soviet expansion may have been due to opportunism rather than global strategy. Thus, presumably, negotiations might play a role in reversing them."[24] Since then, both the Soviet Union and China have actively sought normalization of relations, and there has been some tangible improvement in the economic field. However, this normalization process has not extended to the more critical matters of national security, with regard to which Beijing has stipulated that three "obstacles" to normalization must be removed before there can be progress in substantive relations with Moscow, and even then any Sino-Soviet relationship will continue to be limited in scope and character. This was made explicitly clear by President Li Xiannian when he stated in July 1985: "So long as the three obstacles are not removed, one can hardly think of normalizing Sino-Soviet relations. Even if the three obstacles are removed, the Sino-Soviet relationship will not revert to that of an alliance like the one in the 1950s. China is now determined to follow an independent course of diplomacy; it will not enter into an alliance with one power or another."[25]

The three obstacles that the Chinese want removed—Soviet backing of the Vietnamese invasion of Cambodia, significant numbers of Soviet forces in Mongolia, and the Soviet presence in Afghanistan—are in fact nothing other than intrinsic elements of the Soviet strategy for the containment of China.

Soviet support of Vietnam is not only critical to continued Vietnamese control of Cambodia, as well as the rest of Indochina, but it also provides Moscow with the leverage to create tensions on China's southern flank when it serves Soviet purposes. The Vietnamese have proven themselves capable of being both troublesome and dangerous neighbors and appear prepared to contest China's hegemonic ambitions and claims of sovereignty over the islands and offshore resources in the South China Sea region.

The deployment of large numbers of Soviet forces along the Sino-Soviet and Sino-Mongolian frontiers has long been an essential reflection of Moscow's concern for the security of its extensive lines of communication across Asia. The critical link connecting the Far East with the centers of power in European Russia is the Trans-Siberian Railway, which for some 2,000 miles, from Irkutsk to Khabarovsk, skirts the southern edge of the Siberian permafrost zone. This places the railroad along the northern fringe of the Inner Asian zone of steppes and deserts that stretch along the Sino-Soviet frontier. For approximately 800 miles the railroad is less than 150 miles from Mongolia's northern border. In this region, devoid of natural barriers that would impede an incursion from the south aimed at interrupting the primary Soviet line of communication, such proximity was considered by Soviet military planners as unacceptable. The desired strategic depth was achieved by extending Moscow's sway over Mongolia, effectively moving the frontier away from the railroad to the Sino-Mongolian border.

The railroad's vulnerability has been reduced to some degree by the construction of the Baikal-Amur Main Line, whose tracks in the vicinity of Mongolia run a good distance farther north than the Trans-Siberian. However, the fundamental need to provide security for critical Soviet lines of communication running parallel to a hostile and increasingly militarily capable China for thousands of miles remains a matter of utmost concern. Chinese insistence on a thinning of Soviet forces along the frontier and their withdrawal from Mongolia is nothing less than a demand that the Soviets accept strategic vulnerability in an area intrinsically critical to the security of Asiatic Russia. For the Soviets this would be an extremely high price to pay for only partial normalization of relations between Beijing and Moscow.

Similarly, the matter of the Soviet occupation and control of Afghanistan, as will be discussed later, involves a fundamental Soviet strategic interest that precludes accommodation with Beijing's demands. Suffice it to note at this point that the Soviet position in Afghanistan does indeed serve as a significant challenge to Chinese interests. Soviet occupation and apparent annexation of the Wakhan corridor, which once separated the Soviet Union from Pakistan, poses a serious potential threat both to Pakistan itself, as well as to continued Chinese overland access to Indian Ocean ports through Pakistan. It also gives the Soviets control of the Wakhjir Pass, eliminating the previous direct connection between China and Afghanistan. In the view of one Pakistani defense analyst, "this is the most dangerous thing that has yet happened to Pakistan because it puts the Soviet Union on 180 miles of our border."[26]

By placing Soviet forces within easy striking distance—some 30 miles—the Karakorum Highway, built by China with great effort and expense through the Kunjrab Pass and across territories claimed by India, Moscow is in a position to isolate western China at will. Reports from Beijing indicate the presence of more than 4,000 Soviet troops in the Wakhan corridor. In addition, the Soviets are believed to have built underground bunkers, permanent barracks, and ground-to-ground missile sites, all of which clearly reflect an intention to remain in the Wakhan.[27] Here again, the Chinese have obviously and deliberately set their price for normalization of relations too high for serious positive consideration by the Kremlin.

Moscow is also well aware that any temporary accommodation with Beijing would give China the respite it needs so badly to strengthen and modernize its forces further for a possible confrontation with the Soviet Union in the not too distant future. Under the assumption that there is not a credible threat of nuclear escalation by China in response to a conventional attack by Soviet forces except under conditions of total war, one long-discussed option open to Moscow would be a lightning assault aimed at seizing strategic segments of Chinese territory in order to create a new and extensive buffer zone between central China and Siberia.[28] In the view of Edward N. Luttwak, this possibility must now be given renewed and more serious consideration. He argues that at the level of grand strategy, two premises must underlie any viable war option for Moscow: "that China is not destroyable, and that it cannot be occupied in its totality to be remade to order. . . . This leaves only one feasible goal for a Soviet war: if an independent China of growing power can be neither tolerated nor destroyed, then it must be divided."[29] That is, a feasible solution for the Soviets would be a series of conventional assaults on parts of China that have relatively large non–ethnic Chinese populations, and the subsequent transformation of these territories into client states that would actively resist, presumably with Soviet assistance, reincorporation into China.

This suggests that a Soviet attempt to carve up China would focus primarily on the thinly populated and ethnically mixed regions of Xinjiang, Tibet, Qinghai, northern Gansu, Inner Mongolia, and the northern part of Heilongjiang. These provinces and regions comprise about 56 percent of China's territory, but only about 6 percent of the population, one-third of which is non–ethnic Chinese. Since the rambling Sino-Soviet border is basically indefensible against Soviet attacks, this scenario is quite plausible. Indeed, in the event of a serious Soviet invasion of China, a credible defense perimeter could be drawn only, according to General Wego Chiang (Taiwan), at the waist of the country along a line running from Beijing through Lanzhou in southern Gansu to Tibet.[30] This would in effect cede all the targeted areas to the Soviets. However, Moscow would still have to consider the possibility of China's turning to the United States for the large-scale military aid that could turn the projected surgical operation into a meat grinder.

China, as a regional power, thus presents the Soviet Union with a security challenge that can hardly be dismissed, as well as with the broader geostrategic dilemma noted earlier. These problems are further compounded when China is considered from the perspective of its possible role as a volatile buffer zone in a conventional military confrontation between the Soviet Union and the United States in the Asia-Pacific theater.

The apparent intractability of the China problem has led the Soviets to try to defuse the tensions between the two countries once again. This effort is clearly designed to attempt to head off any close security relationship between China and the United States or its major Asian ally, Japan. On July 28, 1986, Mikhail Gorbachev held out an olive branch to China in a major speech at Vladivostok that reaffirmed the Soviet commitment to the development of Asiatic Russia and its role as an Asian power. On the delicate matter of the Sino-Soviet border, Gorbachev appeared to be extremely conciliatory to China.

We are convinced that the historically established complementarity between the Soviet and the Chinese economies gives great opportunities for expanding these ties, including in the border regions. Some of the major problems of cooperation are literally knocking at the door. For instance, we do not want the border river of Amur to be viewed as a "water obstacle." Let the basin of this mighty river unite the efforts of the Chinese and the Soviet peoples in using for mutual benefit the rich resources available there and for building water management projects. An intergovernmental agreement on this account is being jointly worked out. And the official border might pass along the main ship channel.[31]

It was surely this very last sentence, which reads almost like an afterthought, that made many Chinese officials sit up and take careful notice. If the boundary were to be set along the main ship channel, on the Ussuri River this would mean that the island of Chenbao, the site of the armed clashes of 1969, would be on the Chinese side of the new border. This gesture was seen in Beijing as a possibly significant Soviet concession, even though none of China's major concerns were addressed adequately and some not at all. It was evident from the tone of Gorbachev's speech, if not its substance, that the Kremlin seriously wanted to warm up relations with Beijing. The Gorbachev initiative was soon followed by a peace offensive directed at Beijing. That same month, Gorbachev had sent his chief arms negotiator at the Geneva talks with the United States, Viktor Karpov, to Beijing to advise the Chinese on the Soviet negotiating position.[32] In late August the highest-ranking Soviet official to visit China in 17 years, First Deputy Prime Minister Ivan Archipov, arrived in Beijing ostensibly for acupuncture treatments.[33]

Nonetheless, the Soviets understand quite well that the geopolitical dynamics of the region preclude a real reversal by China of its policy toward the Soviet Union. Internal developments in China indicate movement toward greater assertion of Chinese interests in Asia, which will almost inevitably put it on a collision course with the Soviet Union. Furthermore, any substantive improvement in Sino-Soviet relations, even if only temporary, would likely involve a significant lessening of immediate Soviet concern about the defense of its long frontier with China. This would leave it free to concentrate further on an already alarming military buildup in Northeast Asia. This, in turn, could precipitate a Japanese move toward remilitarization, something that neither the Soviet Union nor China wishes to see. Were this to happen, it would also have a major impact on the balance of power in the Far East, where the Soviet Union must face a U.S. containment line built on substantial naval and air power anchored in Japan, Korea, and the Philippines. This already poses a significant military challenge to Soviet power projection to the eastern periphery of Asia and the Western Pacific. A new major defense buildup by Japan would further exacerbate the Soviet problem in the region. It would also raise the specter of a possible Sino-Japanese alliance that could only be detrimental to Soviet interests in Asia.

Here, as in Europe, Moscow has more to gain by a policy toward the states along the eastern rim of the continent that is designed to undermine the bilateral alliances between the several states and the United States, thereby forestalling the emergence of any mutual security structure involving those countries. The goal is to force the withdrawal of U.S. power from its forward positions in the region through neutralization of the host countries. Toward this end, Moscow is exploiting the acute Japanese sensitivity to the possibility of once again becoming the target of nuclear attack as a consequence of its security arrangement with the United States. The Soviet buildup in Northeast Asia must therefore be carried out in a way that suggests it is not intended against Japan per se, but rather only to ensure the security of Soviet interests in the region in the context of a confrontation with the United States. Were any Soviet moves in the region to be generally perceived in Japan as directed specifically against it, the consequences would be to increase rather than diminish the strategic vulnerabilities faced by Moscow.

Finally, it is of considerable importance to note that on all three of its exposed flanks, Soviet land power is confronted primarily by opposing maritime power. At the same time, it must be recognized that the Soviet Union is the only power that can reach all three areas by means of interior lines of communication. This factor has always been one of major significance for Moscow.

The Soviet Far East

Prior to 1964 the remoteness of the Far East and the lack of an adequate transportation infrastructure linking the region to Soviet markets in Europe inhibited the heavy investments required to exploit its abundant resources. Generally speaking, it was considered uneconomical to pursue large-scale industrial development east of Lake Baikal in Siberia, notwithstanding the wealth of the region in mineral and timber resources. The sole available means of practical transcontinental transportation was the Trans-Siberian Railway, built in the late nineteenth century. Despite its upgrading, including electrification and dual tracking, it remained inadequate to support the effective economic exploitation of the vast region.

Nonetheless, after 1964, as a consequence of planning decisions reached by the Kremlin upon the accession of Leonid Brezhnev to power, the Soviet Union undertook a major industrial development program in the region east of Lake Baikal. This took place in the course of implementation of the 1959–65 Seven-Year Plan, which was predicated on the continued slow pace of investment and development in the region. In fact, the per capita living space in the Far East was expected to drop by 9 percent as compared with the rest of the vast RSFSR, of which it is a part.[34] That the change in direction took place rather suddenly is evidenced by the consideration that even the preliminary economic and geographical research required for an intensive development program in the Far East was not undertaken until the 1960s, after it became evident that Sino-Soviet relations were in a steep downward spiral.

By 1965 fixed capital investment in the region exceeded that of 1960 by some 58 percent. This was a dramatic change from the 1960 figure, which showed an increase of only about 6 percent over such investment in 1958.[35] Furthermore, the population of the Soviet Far East in 1966 showed an increase of 14.6 percent over what it stood at in 1959, compared with a Soviet Union–wide increase of only 11 percent.[36] In July 1967 a special decree, which called for a tripling of industrial output in the region by 1975, was issued outside the framework of the controlling Five-Year Plan. The industries covered included a broad range of linked economic activities such as mining, power and energy, agriculture, fishing, and construction.[37] The pattern of heavy investment has continued over the past two decades, according to some analysts, at a rate six times that of the national average.[38]

In addition, a number of complementary initiatives were undertaken to bolster the development of the Soviet Far East. One was designed to attract and retain immigrants to the region. Another 1967 decree extended benefits formerly provided exclusively to workers in heavy industry to those engaged in a wide range of activities, and it included pay increases over time to encourage long-term job commitment. A second initiative established the Far East Science Center in 1970, which incorporated a number of existing regional institutes and employed more than 5,000 by 1975. According to Robert N. North, "it can be seen as a step towards the decentralization of scientific talent from Moscow and Leningrad, analogous to the better-known creation of Akademgorodok near Novosibirsk in West Siberia."[39]

The "Project of the Century"

As an intrinsic component of the Far East development program, in 1974 the Soviets began construction of what they called the "project of the century," the Baikal-Amur Mainline (BAM), a new 2,000-mile-long railroad reaching into the heart of the inhospitable and relatively inaccessible region. This monumental project brought the railroad across 5 mountain ranges and 17 rivers, through 4 tunnels, one of which is more than nine miles long, and over 58 bridges especially constructed for it. In addition, a major branch line, the "little BAM," was built to provide a connection to the BAM from the Yakutian coal fields, for the purpose of transporting coking coal to Soviet Pacific ports for export.[40]

The initial requirement for the BAM resulted from strategic military decisions, originally made by Stalin sometime in the early 1930s, which were apparently long kept secret. The construction of the line was supposed to be "under the direct auspices of the N.K.V.D." and had been "shrouded in mystery since 1934."[41] The Kremlin was clearly concerned about the growing strength of Japan and its aggressive behavior in Manchuria. This led the Soviet leaders to consider means of overcoming the serious deficiencies of the Trans-Siberian Railway in order to meet the military supply needs of large numbers of troops operating in the Far East.[42] It was clear that those inadequacies were a major factor contributing to Russia's defeat in the Russo-Japanese War (1904–5).

Actual construction of the BAM originally began in 1939 but was abandoned in 1941 because of the war in Europe. The decision to proceed with construction again came only after the rift between Moscow and Beijing assumed its clearly geopolitical dimensions in 1964. Preliminary work on the new railroad began in 1965 with the construction of two short sections at opposite ends of the line. One was an extension of the Trans-Siberian Railway from Taishet to Ust'-Kut, a port on the Lena River, and the other a line from Komsomolsk on the Amur River eastward to the port of Sovetskaya Gavan on the Tatar Strait. Both sections were completed by 1968.[43] Construction of the 3,150-kilometer main trunk of the BAM, between Ust'-Kut and Komsomolsk, began in 1974 and was completed in September 1984, with upgrading and spur line construction continuing at this writing. In early 1985, construction of the new 830-kilometer Amur-Yakutsk Railway connecting Yakutsk with both the Trans-Siberian and the BAM was announced. Completion of that project is expected in 1995.[44]

Because this railroad parallels the Trans-Siberian along much of the section where the latter is quite close to the Sino-Soviet border, although located approximately 100–300 miles farther north, it has been viewed by some as intended primarily to support military operations in the region in the event of a war with China. In this view, the primary purpose of the BAM is to provide additional and more secure transcontinental transportation capability. Though such a perspective is plausible, it is seriously flawed. This becomes evident when one considers that the BAM extends westward from its main Far Eastern junction at Komsomolsk on the Amur River for about 2,000 miles until it connects with the Trans-Siberian Railway at Taishet, about 500 miles west of Lake Baikal. Since the Trans-Siberian is already very heavily used from this junction point westward toward European Russia and is double tracked and electrified only between Moscow and Irkutsk,[45] any significant increase in freight traffic to or from the Far East would severely overtax its capabilities. The Trans-Siberian, as is the case with Soviet railroads generally, to meet the demands of extensive and rapid industrialization east of the Urals over the last two decades, is already working at or near maximum capacity.[46] Indeed, as argued by Gregory Copley, "major Soviet deployment to the Far East and the Pacific cannot be supported using the logistical capacity of the Trans-Siberian Railroad. That system, even with the new BAM spur, is insufficient to sustain anything like the needs of the Soviet Far East in times of peace, let alone in time of conflict.''[47] A recent Chinese estimate indicates that the annual military transportation capacity of the Trans-Siberian Railway in peacetime is about 40 million tons, and no more than 60 million tons in wartime. The BAM is expected to augment this capacity by about 30 million tons.[48]

An alternative and probably more realistic perception is that the BAM was built at extraordinary expense (it is estimated to have cost three times that of the U.S. Trans-Alaskan Pipeline)[49] primarily to facilitate the exploitation of the region's vast coal and timber resources and not to provide increased transcontinental railroad capacity. According to V. Gorbunov, the BAM is expected to contribute significantly to the integration of some 1.5 million square kilometers of resource-rich territory into the Soviet economy.[50] In addition, the BAM is intended to facilitate the expansion of steel production and export in the Soviet Far East based on the use of the iron ore and coking coal of the Aldan region.[51] Since, as was noted above, it is impracticable to transport these bulk resources across the continent by rail, this suggests that the purpose of the railroad is to connect the interior with seaports on the Pacific coast of Siberia.[52] In other words, this very significant increase in *regional* railroad capacity will impose a dramatically increased demand for maritime transport between Soviet Asian ports and the nearest Soviet European ports in the Black Sea.

The Transition to Waterways

Parallel to their decisions on development in eastern Siberia, the Soviets have also made the basic decision to begin to shift Eurasian transcontinental and interregional transport from railroads to seaways and pipelines. From the mid 1960s to 1983, the percentage of total freight turnover handled by railroad in the Soviet Union declined from 83 to 58 percent. During the same period maritime freight doubled from 7 to 14 percent and it continues to rise.[53] It seems reasonably clear that the bulk of this maritime traffic is between Soviet ports in Europe and Asia. In 1978 the West German military and national intelligence service (BND) estimated that 80 percent of Soviet freight transported across the continent went via the southern sea route rather than overland by rail.[54]

It is noteworthy that of the 20 major ports in the world, the greatest percentage of expansion has been taking place in the Soviet Far East, at Vladivostok, Nakhodka, and Petropavlovsk, followed by port development in the Black Sea.[55] In addition, the Soviets are extending the deep-water all-weather port at Vostochny, near Vladivostok, which is planned to be the largest container-handling port in the world.

The southern sea route from Soviet Black Sea ports to Vladivostok via the Suez Canal is approximately 11,000 miles and takes a freighter traveling at an average speed of 14 nautical miles per hour about 32 days to complete the voyage. The alternate route through the Strait of Gibraltar and around Africa, which was the only route available from 1967 to 1975, when the Suez Canal was closed, is approximately 17,000 miles and takes 50 days. It is noteworthy that the shipment of bulk freight over the longer alternate route is still more cost-effective than the use of the much shorter and faster railroad across Asia.

The full implications of the Soviet decision to develop the Far Eastern territories both economically and militarily have yet to be adequately understood and assessed. We are witnessing a fundamental change in the traditional pattern of communications that bears far-reaching geopolitical consequences. At the point where the Soviet Union becomes heavily dependent on sea lines of communication, its security posture becomes fundamentally altered.[56] For the first time in its history, the Soviet Union must begin to rely on exterior lines of communication over which it cannot as yet exercise effective control. This is a situation that Moscow cannot long tolerate.

Soviet vulnerability in this regard was brought home very sharply in 1969, when China blocked overland shipments of supplies from the Soviet Union to Vietnam. This meant that Moscow had to use the long sea route around Africa to supply Vietnam in its war with the United States at a time when, from a strictly military standpoint, the United States could have interdicted such shipments at will.

The Soviet Union must, if it is to continue to pursue its global geopolitical aspirations, take the steps necessary to overcome this obvious strategic liability. Though the growth in Soviet naval power is being observed carefully and with concern in the Far East as well as among the members of the Western alliance, its broader geopolitical implications have not yet been sufficiently appreciated by contemporary statesmen and strategists. Throughout its history a major land power, the Soviet Union is now in the process of becoming a major sea power. This was clearly signaled by Admiral Sergei Gorshkov in 1972.

And today abroad there is widespread propaganda produced by American ideologists asserting that the Soviet state does not need a powerful navy. An example of this is President Nixon's speech of 4 August 1970 in which he stated: "That which the Soviet Union needs in way of military preparations differs from what we need. The USSR is a land power . . . while we are primarily a sea power . . . "

One hardly has to say that this speech of Nixon's . . . bears no relationship to the actual state of affairs and contradicts the interests of our state both past and present.[57]

As an emerging world-class maritime power, the Soviet Union is confronted by serious geostrategic liabilities that it would not have to face as a land power. As was observed by Soviet Admiral V. V. Sidorov, "the open ocean effectiveness of Soviet naval forces is adversely affected by geographic constraints on their operations. . . . The four Soviet fleets—Northern, Baltic, Black Sea, and Pacific—are widely separated and must either traverse considerable distances or transit through choke points to reach the open ocean."[58] Its northern sea route westward must pass along the coast of Norway and then through the Greenland–Iceland–United Kingdom gap, a 1,500 mile passage dominated by the navies and air forces of NATO. Furthermore, to keep the northern sea route open in winter, the Soviet navy depends on the northern end of the Gulf Stream flow to carve a channel between the coast and the Arctic ice pack that reaches south of Svalbard and then runs parallel to the Kola Peninsula for some 180 miles east to Svyatoy Nos, about 240 miles from the Norwegian border. NATO has taken advantage of this situation to establish near the North Cape a sophisticated sound surveillance system that monitors Soviet ship movements from the Norwegian coast to Bear Island.[59]

The northern route eastward, from Murmansk and Archangel to Vladivostok, is open only about 100 days a year because of Arctic ice. In the Far East, the ice pack descends east of Kamchatka and the Kurile Islands and as far south as Hokkaido and then west to the mouth of the bay at Vladivostok. Vladivostok is icebound for three months a year and averages 85 days of fog. Sovetskaya Gavan, on the Tatar Strait opposite Sakhalin, is icebound from December to March, and Petropavlovsk on Kamchatka is also frozen in for three to four months a year. Nonetheless, all these ports can be kept open by icebreakers, and Moscow is beginning to take steps to keep this route open for a longer period by an accelerated investment in heavy icebreaker vessels.

From their Baltic ports, Soviet ships must pass through the very narrow and easily mined NATO-controlled Danish Straits flanked by Norway, Denmark, Sweden, and West Germany before reaching the open seas in an area also dominated by NATO forces.

From its Black Sea terminals the Soviet southern sea route must pass through the very narrow (at some points only three-quarters of a mile wide) and easily mined Turkish Straits and then either through the Suez Canal choke point or the NATO-dominated Mediterranean and Strait of Gibraltar before even beginning the long oceanic passage to the Far East. Even then the southern sea route must pass through the Strait of Malacca or one of the Indonesian straits before entering the South China Sea. This entire area is within the operational range of the substantial U.S. naval and air forces located in the Philippines.

Most of the major Soviet industrial ports in Asia are located on the Sea of Japan, which is effectively a closed sea with outlets only through the Tatar, Soya, Tsugaru, Tsushima, and Korea straits, the last four of which are at present fully susceptible to Japanese and U.S. control. Finally, though elements of the Pacific fleet based at Petropavlovsk on the Kamchatka Peninsula have easy direct access to the Pacific Ocean, the base is difficult to support logistically because of its remoteness from supply centers in the Soviet Union. Thus the ability to sustain naval operations out of Petropavlovsk is largely contingent upon the reliable and unimpeded use of the northern and, most especially, the southern sea routes.

Increased Soviet reliance on the southern sea route to meet its Far Eastern needs also means that the Soviet navy must deploy a good part of its assets to protect its shipping in both the Atlantic and Pacific oceans, thus limiting the naval forces available for offensive operations. And, as has been pointed out, a good part of the Soviet fleet is not actually deployed for the protection of logistic traffic. This means that such traffic is underprotected and therefore seriously exposed to interdiction.[60]

Though the Soviet Union's strategic posture in East Asia is enhanced somewhat by its occupation of the Kurile Islands north of Japan and the former U.S. bases at Cam Ranh Bay and Danang in Vietnam, at the present time these forward positions cannot be effectively exploited to reduce significantly the vulnerability of the southern sea route. The air and maritime lines of communication from Soviet mainland Pacific bases to Vietnam stretch for some 2,000 miles through sectors where they are intrinsically vulnerable, such as the Japanese Straits, the Taiwan Strait, or the Bashi Channel. At each of these choke points, the United States is presently capable of deploying far superior naval forces than the Soviet Union. Furthermore, whereas the Soviet lines of communication run north-south along the Asian coast, the U.S. lines of communication to support forward deployment in the region follow multiple east-west courses that intersect the Soviet routes perpendicularly at points on the eastern rim of Asia.

The U.S. lines of communication, although longer than those of the Soviet Union, are nonetheless more secure because of the vast room for defensive maneuver in the open ocean and airspace of the Pacific in contrast to the lines of communications passing through the more confined coastal channels along the periphery of the continent.[61] The maintenance of the U.S. advantage in strategic position in Asia is thus largely dependent on its continued capacity to project power from its present Philippine bases. Should the United States lose the Subic Bay and Clark bases, much of the vulnerability in the Soviet geostrategic posture in East Asia would be mitigated. Should those bases ever come under Soviet control, in conjunction with the Soviet forward position in Vietnam, the balance of power in Asia could shift decisively in favor of Moscow, forcing the regional states including China to make accommodations that are today virtually unthinkable.

Notes

1. Milan Hauner, "Seizing the Third Parallel: Geopolitics and the Soviet Advance into Central Asia," *Orbis*, Spring 1985, p. 31.

2. A. Ross Johnson, "The Warsaw Pact: Soviet Military Policy in Eastern Europe," in Sarah Meiklejohn Terry, ed., *Soviet Policy in Eastern Europe*, p. 278.

3. Edward B. Atkeson, "The 'Fault Line' in the Warsaw Pact: Implications for NATO Strategy," *Orbis*, Spring 1986, p. 116.

4. Colin Gray, "Keeping the Soviets Landlocked: Geostrategy for a Maritime America," *National Interest*, Summer 1986, p. 36.

5. Seth Cropsey, "Forward Defense Or Maginot Line?" *Policy Review*, Fall 1986, p. 41.

6. Milan Vego, "The Soviet Envelopment Option on the Northern Flank," *Naval War College Review*, Autumn 1986, pp. 32–33.

7. Fred Halliday, *Soviet Policy in the Arc of Crisis*, p. 36.

8. Albert E. Graham, "Soviet Strategy and Policy in the Indian Ocean," in Paul J. Murphy, ed., *Naval Power in Soviet Policy*, p. 276.

9. Selig S. Harrison, "Cut a Regional Deal," *Foreign Policy*, Spring 1986, p. 127.

10. John J. Stephan, "Asia in the Soviet Conception," in Donald S. Zagoria, *Soviet Policy in East Asia*, p. 31.

11. Cited by W. A. Douglas Jackson, *The Russo-Chinese Borderlands*, pp. 116–17.

12. *New York Times*, September 7, 1963; *Christian Science Monitor*, October 2, 1963.

13. Cited by O. Edmund Clubb, *China and Russia: The "Great Game"*, p. 496.

14. Ibid., pp. 497–98.

15. Z. Mieczowski, "The Soviet Far East: Problem Region of the USSR," *Pacific Affairs*, Summer 1968, p. 226.

16. Cited by Robert Guillain, *Le Monde*, March 18, 1969.

17. Richard C. Thornton, "Strategic Change and American Foreign Policy: Perceptions of the Sino-Soviet Conflict," *Journal of Northeast Asian Studies*, Spring 1986, p. 53.

18. *Pravda*, June 7, 1969.

19. Radio Moscow, March 7, 1973 (Foreign Broadcast Information Service [FBIS], *Daily Report: Soviet Union*).

20. Clifton C. Carpenter, "The Inner Asian Frontier: A Cradle of Conflict," *Strategic Review*, Winter 1977, pp. 91–96.

21. Cited by Richard A. Pierce, *Russian Central Asia, 1867–1917*, p. 298.

22. Edgar O'Ballance, "Gorbachev's Thoughts on China," *Asian Defence Journal*, October 1985, p. 94.

23. *Xinhua News Bulletin*, September 24, 1981.

24. Carol Lee Hamrin, "China Reassesses the Superpowers," *Pacific Affairs*, Summer 1983, p. 222.

25. Cited in International Security Council, *The United States, China and the Soviet Union: Strategic Dilemmas and Options*, p. 6.

26. Noor A. Husain, director general of the Institute of Strategic Studies of Islamabad, cited by William J. Coughlin, "Soviets Quietly Annex Strategic Afghan Turf," *Washington Times*, November 10, 1986.

27. Coughlin, op. cit.

28. Thomas W. Robinson, "Soviet Policy in East Asia," *Problems of Communism*, November-December 1973, p. 49.

29. Edward N. Luttwak, *The Grand Strategy of the Soviet Union*, pp. 102ff.

30. Wego W. K. Chiang, *The Strategic Significance of Taiwan*, p. 71.

31. "Mikhail Gorbachyov on International Affairs," *Soviet Daily News* (USSR Embassy, Peking), July 30, 1986, p. 9.

32. *Times* (London), August 17, 1986.

33. *Financial Times*, August 22, 1986.

34. Z. Mieczowski, "The Soviet Far East: Problem Region of the USSR," *Pacific Affairs*, Summer 1968, p. 223.

35. Ibid., p. 224.

36. Ibid., p. 225.

37. Robert N. North, "The Soviet Far East: New Centre of Attention in the U.S.S.R.," *Pacific Affairs*, Summer 1978, p. 198.

38. James T. Westwood, "The Soviet Union and the Southern Sea Route," *Naval War College Review*, January-February 1982, p. 58.

39. North, op. cit., pp. 199–200.

40. Theodore Shabad and Victor L. Mote, *Gateway to Siberian Resources*, p. 52.

41. V. Conolly, *Soviet Asia*, p. 13.

42. C. Bohlen, "Soviets Lay Last Rail in New Far East Link," *Washington Post*, September 30, 1984; K. Ebata, "The Second Siberian Railway," *Jane's Defence Weekly*, March 16, 1985, p. 443.

43. Michael Dankewych, *Siberia in Global Power Politics: Economic, Strategic and Geographical Factors*, p. 66.

44. *Xinhua News Bulletin*, April 13, 1985.

45. O. S. Nock, *World Atlas of Railways*, p. 93.

46. R. N. Taaffe and R. C. Kingsbury, *An Atlas of Soviet Affairs*, p. 120.

47. Gregory Copley, "Why Moscow Looks to the South," *Defense and Foreign Affairs*, February 1985, p. 13.

48. *Beijing Review*, March 25, 1985.

49. Shabad and Mote, op. cit., p. 67.

50. V. Gorbunov, "Our Dialogues: Building and Running the Baikal-Amur Mainline Railroad," *Socialist Industry*, January 15, 1985; V. Gorbunov, "The Mainland of the Future," *Pravda*, June 13, 1984.

51. Robert W. Campbell, "Prospects for Siberian Economic Development," in Donald S. Zagoria, *Soviet Policy in East Asia*, p. 249.

52. James T. Westwood, "Soviet Maritime Strategy and Transportation," *Naval War College Review*, November-December 1985, p. 49.

53. John L. Scherer, ed., *USSR Facts and Figures Annual*, vol. 10, p. 241.

54. Westwood, "Soviet Maritime Strategy," p. 47.

55. James T. Westwood, "The Soviet Union and the Southern Sea Route," *Naval War College Review*, January-February 1982, p. 61.

56. Ibid., p. 63.

57. Cited by Abram N. Shulsky, "Gorshkov on Naval Arms Limitations: KTO KOGO?", in Paul J. Murphy, ed., *Naval Power in Soviet Policy*, p. 254.

58. Cited by Anthony H. Cordesman, "The Western Naval Threat to Soviet Military Dominance: A *Soviet* Assessment," *Armed Forces Journal International*, April 1983. (Reprinted in part in U.S. Department of Defense, *Current News: Special Edition*, no. 996, May 3, 1983, p. 12.)

59. Pierre Gallois, "The Kola Peninsula and Its Strategic Importance," *Journal of Defense and Diplomacy*, September 1986, p. 40.

60. Copley, op. cit., p. 13.

61. Marc A. Moore, "Power Projection Strategy along East Asian Rimlands," *Marine Corps Gazette*, December 1986, p. 16.

7   The Emerging Strategy

The Soviet Union, a "heartland" power in classical geopolitical terminology, must become a "rimland" power if it is to be capable of competing effectively with the maritime alliances of the West for dominance over the world's critical sea lines of communication. Thus, the attainment of strategically significant positions along the peripheries of Africa and Asia becomes an integral component of Soviet security strategy. From such positions the Soviets would be better able to project the power necessary to secure their increasingly important but highly vulnerable exterior lines of communication between Europe and Asia. Moscow would then also be in a better position to transform those lines into a security belt around China that could be tightened at will. The Soviet Union began to implement this strategy of forward deployment after the Twenty-third CPSU Congress, when its navy was directed to move into the hostile maritime environment dominated by the West and demonstrate the growing Soviet capability for power projection in support of its global interests.[1]

There is sound strategic logic in the Soviet determination to establish a dominating position in the Indian Ocean. It washes the shores of most of the countries of the Middle East, which is an area of intrinsic geostrategic importance to the Soviet Union. It also provides the connecting maritime link between Soviet forward positions in the Mediterranean, Red, and Arabian seas and in the Pacific Ocean. The Suez Canal, although not heavily used by Soviet warships, as opposed to its extensive use by Soviet merchant vessels, nonetheless provides an important link between the Black Sea and Pacific fleets. Furthermore, the vulnerability of the Trans-Siberian Railway to interdiction or even seizure by the Chinese in the event of hostilities with the Soviet Union leaves sea and airlift as the only viable options available to Moscow for meeting its military and civilian needs in the Far East. For this reason alone, the sea lines of communication passing through the Indian Ocean are of ever greater importance to the internal cohesion of the Soviet Union. Thus, V. Kudryavtsev emphasized as early as 1974, "these sea communications are very important to the Soviet Union since they represent the only non-freezing sea-route linking Soviet ports in the Black and Azov seas with Soviet ports in the Far East."[2] In an unusually candid statement, Moscow took this argument concerning the criticality of the southern sea route, particularly the passage through the Indian Ocean, a step farther in 1980 by indicating quite clearly that it considered its possible control by others as a direct challenge to Soviet national security. "The escalation of U.S. military might in this region cannot fail to be regarded . . . as a threat to the security of the Soviet Union . . . which uses the Indian Ocean as the only non-freezing sea route uniting two of its parts—the European and the Far Eastern regions."[3]

Soviet strategy in the Indian Ocean is thus designed both to influence the foreign and national security policies of the littoral states in ways favorable to Soviet interests, and to control the critical sea lines of communication between Europe, the Middle East, and the Pacific. The Soviet effort to implement such a strategy was inaugurated by the February 1968 visit of Admiral Sergei Gorshkov to India. Presumably, he sought to obtain rights for Soviet warships to be refueled and repaired at Indian naval facilities. Since then, the Soviet Union has repeatedly attempted to gain access to naval facilities of one kind or another in a number of Indian Ocean littoral states. As has been noted by Albert E. Graham, "while no overt official treaty exists guaranteeing formal base rights in any Indian Ocean state, the Soviet Union has constructed major naval facilities for host nations, thus sometimes creating facilities for use by her own Navy. The informal nature of the facilities enjoyed by Moscow in a number of Indian Ocean harbors permits it to deny having bases at all."[4]

Since the 1970s the Soviet Union has actively pursued a rimland strategy along the entire length of its southern sea route. One of the initial goals of this strategy appears to be to reduce its vulnerability by establishing sufficient positions of air and naval strength along the route to deny sea control to the Western maritime powers acting singly or in concert. Thus, as expressed by the *Soviet Military Encyclopedia*, the current mission of the Soviet navy is to act as a "restraining factor against the unleashing of a new world war by the aggressive forces of imperialism."[5] That is, its primary mission today is to challenge the ability of the maritime alliances of the West to exercise effective control of the seas for strategic purposes that are opposed to Soviet security interests. A concomitant of this mission is the capacity to prevent other powers from interfering in the Soviet Union's unimpeded use of the sea for its own purposes. In explaining the predominant characteristics of the Soviet naval force posture, a former U.S. chief of naval operations, Admiral James L. Holloway, observed a decade ago: "If you look at the Soviet's geography, not only are all their principal allies connected to them by overland routes but their two principal enemies are on the same continent with them—China in Asia and the NATO countries in Europe. So their navy is designed for one thing: to prevent the United States from exercising its influence abroad in support of our allies and our national interests. Therefore they have an interdictory type of navy— ships like submarines, aircraft with antiship missiles to sink ships."[6]

Presumably, once the denial of sea control by others is assured, Moscow will be in a position to seek such strategic domination itself. Indeed, as was noted with regret by Soviet Admiral Vladimir V. Si- dorov, "had the US continued its strategic drift of the 1970s, the Soviet navy might well be on the way to controlling the seas in many regions and denying the West its use of maritime routes in a crisis or war."[7] In other words, notwithstanding the vagaries of the timetable, which is subject to continual alteration as a result of actions taken by the United States, the basic Soviet strategy that appears to be emerging is one of hemispheric denial to non-Eurasian powers, that is, to the United States. With the United States excluded from a geopolitical presence in the eastern hemisphere, the Soviet Union would be free to establish its hegemony over both Eurasia and Africa.

Another important facet of Soviet maritime strategy is the attempt to gain control of some of the world's major maritime choke points. This would enable Moscow not only to facilitate the interdiction mission of its naval forces, but also to derive compensation to some extent for the strategic disabilities it currently suffers both in Europe, where all the major maritime choke points are under NATO control, and in the Far East, where access to and from the main Soviet ports can be sealed by Japan. As has been noted by Jack V. Roome, control of the maritime choke points is a highly effective way of carrying out an interdiction mission.

Interdicting merchant sea lines of communications (SLOC) constitutes a Soviet wartime task. Consistent with the recent trend in Soviet thinking about preparing to fight wars which could be protracted during the conventional phase, Soviet naval writings continue to cite the importance of SLOC interdiction.

The vast number of peninsulas and islands in the Pacific zone of Asia results in several compulsory passage points which loom large in the strategy of the world's maritime powers. The two focal points are: in the north, the Japanese straits, which control access by the Soviet Pacific Fleet to the high seas, and in the south, the Malacca, Singapore and Indonesia straits, which link the Pacific and Indian oceans. Many routes are possible through this maze of islands, but only a few can readily be taken by ocean-going vessels.[8]

In addition to the major buildup of forces in Northeast Asia, presumably to enable Moscow to cope with the strategic problems it faces in the Sea of Japan, the Soviets appear to have directed their attentions particularly to those states that guard or border on the strategic entrances to the Indian Ocean. Today, by virtue of its position in both South Yemen and Ethiopia, Moscow is in effective control of the Bab-al-Mandeb Strait. This means that the Soviets can now control access to and from the Suez Canal and Red Sea from the south, just as NATO can control access from the north. Moscow also planned to seek control of the even more critical Strait of Hormuz leading into the Persian Gulf. The blossoming Soviet-Iraqi relationship, which was formalized in a treaty of friendship in 1972, had provided for access to the Iraqi ports of Umm Qasr and Basrah at the northern end of the gulf. In addition, the Soviets had backed the unsuccessful Dhofar rebellion against Oman, which controls one side of Hormuz. Soviet plans for establishing a dominant position in this vital waterway were well under way when they were stymied as an unintended consequence of the outbreak of the Iraq-Iran War and the effective closure of Umm Qasr.

Most serious analysts would agree that, except in a general war situation, it is highly unlikely that the Soviets would attempt to interfere directly with the flow of oil from the Persian Gulf to Europe. It is therefore equally unlikely that Moscow would expend the resources, both material and political, that would be required to place itself in a position to do so effectively. Nonetheless, the generally held view of Soviet attempts to establish positions along the coasts of Africa continues to attribute these endeavors primarily to Moscow's wish to be in a position to threaten the interruption of the flow of oil, and possibly strategic minerals as well, to Europe. This is seen as the only plausible strategic purpose that is served by these moves. However, this perception fails to recognize the critical need for Moscow to reduce the extreme vulnerability of its own economic lifeline to Asiatic Russia. Furthermore, it seems quite clear that the Soviet Union is reasonably well postured to interdict oil traffic from the Persian Gulf region from its already established positions in the Gulf of Aden and the Arabian Sea. For this purpose it would not seem to require bases and facilities in West Africa.

That the Soviets are engaged in a long-term, complex effort to bolster their historic transition from a continental land power to a global sea power is evidenced by what they have already achieved in this regard in little more than a decade of pursuing a rimland strategy. The importance of this transition is also seen by some as reflected in the unprecedented elevation of two fleet admirals, V. V. Sidorov, commander of the Pacific Red Flag Fleet, and I. M. Kapitanyets, commander of the Northern Red Flag Fleet, to be full voting members of the Soviet party Central Committee. This distinction was formerly held only by the commander-in-chief of the navy, Admiral Sergei Gorshkov.[9].

It has been said that the best way to defeat an adversary is by defeating his strategy. However, to do so, one must be aware of what that strategy is.

The Middle East and Mediterranean

By 1964 the Soviets decided to begin the buildup of a permanent naval presence in the Mediterranean as part of a larger political and military design. Prior to this period, the mission of the navy was primarily to support army operations. In the Brezhnev era, however, this began to change significantly. So much so, in fact, that by 1968 the Soviet naval presence became a matter of some concern in Turkey. A government newspaper asked: "What are those Soviet vessels looking for in a sea where they have no coast? The Russians are trying to establish a net throughout the Mediterranean to control the area."[10]

The strength of the Soviet position in this noncontiguous region has long been inversely related to the extent of the Western, particularly the U.S., naval forces operating there. Accordingly, much of Soviet strategy in the region has been designed to promote the withdrawal or reduction of such forces while increasing its own. One aspect of this strategy has been the on-again, off-again promotion of naval limitations in the Mediterranean.

During the Khrushchev era, between the late 1950s and mid 1960s, a common theme of Soviet declarations on the question of security in the Mediterranean was the call for its designation as a denuclearized "zone of peace." This position was a clear reflection of Moscow's concern over the strategic threat posed by the Sixth Fleet and over the inability of its own Mediterranean squadron to offer a credible countervailing challenge to NATO forces operating in the region. However, as a consequence of the Egyptian defeat in the June 1967 war with Israel, the Soviet Union was able to improve its position in the region significantly by gaining access to Egyptian naval facilities for its Mediterranean squadron. With the prospect of a regional base for the further expansion of its naval presence in the Mediterranean, the ardor of the Soviet interest in its own "zone of peace" proposal diminished considerably.[11] When questioned about how Moscow could reconcile the proposal for a "zone of peace" with its naval buildup, Andrei Gromyko responded with the argument that the presence of Soviet warships in the Mediterranean served the interests of peace in the region. He suggested that the Soviet Union, which he considered a Mediterranean country, had a natural and intense interest in preserving peace and security in an area so close to its borders.[12]

On June 11, 1971, in an apparent deviation from the Gromyko line, Leonid Brezhnev stated that the Soviet Union was prepared "to discuss any proposals" that might help bring to an end the less than "ideal situation when navies of the great powers are cruising about for long periods far from their own shores."[13] However, there is reason to believe that Brezhnev's offer had little to do with the resurrection of the proposal for creating a "zone of peace" in the Mediterranean. It was probably more directly related to the Soviet effort to get U.S. ships armed with nuclear weapons systems to be categorized as "forward based systems" within the context of the SALT negotiations taking place at the time.[14]

By 1974, however, as Cairo began to edge toward a new relationship with Washington in the wake of the October War with Israel, the Soviet position in Egypt deteriorated dramatically. This was reflected in April by Anwar Sadat's statement that the status of Soviet access to Egyptian naval facilities was "under discussion."[15] Consequently, Brezhnev soon returned to the "zone of peace" theme. On July 21, in a speech before the Polish parliament, he called specifically for the "withdrawal of ships carrying nuclear weapons" from the Mediterranean.[16] The theme was then amplified by Soviet President Podgorny on September 9 of that same year, when he stated that: "the Soviet Union advocates the turning of the Mediterranean into a zone free of nuclear weapons and into a zone of peace. This would be promoted by the withdrawal of ships with nuclear weapons on board from the Mediterranean region."[17] At the same time, the Soviets intensified their search for alternate naval facilities in the region.

In May 1975, Egypt sharply curtailed Soviet access to its naval facilities. Soviet combat vessels were denied entrance to the harbors at Mersa Matruh and Sollum. They continued to use the anchorage near Sollum but had to remain outside Egyptian territorial waters. Although the Soviet support vessels stationed at Alexandria were permitted to remain there, and the maintenance and repair of submarines was permitted to continue in the shipyards, the Soviets no longer had the freedom of unrestricted movement in or out of the harbor.

It was not long before some of the naval support activities that had previously been carried out in Egypt were transferred to Syria, which now took on new significance as a Soviet client state. In addition, there were consistent reports from the region that the Soviets had been granted unannounced access to Libyan facilities even before Cairo abrogated the Soviet-Egyptian treaty of friendship and cooperation in March 1976.[18] The Soviets also began to make maximum permitted use of ship repair facilities in Yugoslavia.[19] It seems evident, as suggested by Karen Dawisha, that "the continued interest of the Soviet navy in obtaining deep-sea ports has to be seen as a prime motivator of Soviet policy in the Middle East."[20]

As the Egyptian-Soviet relationship approached its end, Libyan-Soviet relations began to blossom. In the same month in which Egypt began to curtail sharply Soviet access to its ports and facilities, Soviet Prime Minister Alexei Kosygin arrived in Tripoli for his first visit to Libya. Soon thereafter, Soviet arms and military advisers began pouring into the country. After Muammar Qaddafi's reciprocal visit to Moscow in December 1976, Libya started to become a potentially significant strategic asset for the Soviet Union. The Soviets began laying the groundwork for transforming Libya into a major base in the very heart of the Mediterranean region. Yosef Bodansky recounted: "Since 1976, the Soviet Union has been constructing a huge military infrastructure in Libya, intended first and foremost for Soviet use. Air bases were refurbished and construction was started on a new base—Banbah— which entered operational use at the end of 1979. Military docking facilities capable of servicing Soviet equipment were installed in most Libyan ports. The large dockyards and Soviet bases are in Benghazi and in Tripoli."[21]

In February 1983 it was reported that the Soviets had just completed a 14,000-foot runway at a military airfield at Jufrah, some 200 miles south of the Mediterranean coast. It was widely assumed that this new facility was specifically designed to accommodate the strategic Backfire bomber, in addition to serving as a base for monitoring NATO installations and operations in Sicily, Greece, and Turkey.[22] The following month, the Soviets reported that Prime Minister Tikhonov had reached agreement with Libya's Abdel Salem Jalloud "to coordinate their efforts in the international arena, in the cause of repelling imperialist aggression."[23]

The air and naval bases available in Libya can provide the Soviets with the facilities from which to project power against NATO's southern flank, and to challenge NATO domination of the Mediterranean and its critical sea lanes. These bases have already served as refueling stops for Soviet airlifts of men and equipment to the African rimland states of Mozambique and Angola.

As has been noted, the Soviets also began to tighten their relations with Syria. In doing so they followed their typical approach to pursuing such ties in the Third World; that is, through the medium of military assistance, which sometimes directly serves Soviet military purposes in addition to those of the recipient country. Thus, when Syrian forces in Lebanon were severely mauled by the Israelis in 1982, the Soviets initially moved rather slowly to resupply their ostensible ally. Then, in 1983, they unaccountably provided the Syrians with SAM–5 missiles, the first time such weaponry had been deployed outside the Soviet bloc. When the early reports of the missile battery installations indicated that one was placed as far north as Mesken, east of Aleppo and relatively far from the Syrian-Israeli frontier, it raised the question as to whether the missile deployment had purposes other than bolstering Syrian defenses against Israeli air power.

It may well have been more than a mere coincidence that the deployment of the SAM–5s took place almost simultaneously with the decision by Turkey to expand the air bases at Erzurum and Batman in the eastern part of the country, as well to construct a new facility between the two at Mus. The avowed purpose of the bases, which are to be made available to NATO or the United States, is to support a war effort that may be required as a consequence of Soviet adventurism in the Middle East. The location of the bases clearly reflects the expectation that such a Soviet move would most likely be directed against Iran and the Persian Gulf. Were the Soviets to conclude that the time was ripe for intervention in Iran, they would thus be faced by a large Turkish army on their right flank supported by substantial air power operating out of these forward bases in eastern Turkey.

The SAM–5, with an operational slant range of some 250 kilometers, is useful primarily to interdict long-range reconnaissance and battle management aircraft such as the AWACS, Hawkeye, and the British Nimrod, thereby limiting the capacity of an opposing force to maintain effective air superiority. The deployment in northern Syria placed operations from the U.S. air base at Incirlik within effective missile range. With the Erzurum base already in range of missile installations at Batum in Soviet Georgia, and an additional swath of Turkish airspace under the shadow of such installations at Yerevan in Soviet Armenia, the Syrian deployment would further reduce the operational ability of the United States or its allies to maintain the control of the airspace over eastern Turkey necessary to support Turkish ground forces in a possible confrontation with the Soviets in Iran. Indeed, it would have required only an additional missile installation at Al-Qamisli in northeastern Syria to provide coverage of all of eastern Turkey to a depth of more than 400 kilometers.

The Syrian-Israeli confrontation thus presented the Kremlin with the occasion for a bold strategic move in anticipation of a Soviet decision to drive through Iran to gain a secure foothold on the Persian Gulf or Indian Ocean coasts. Since 1983 the Soviets have continued to provide large quantities of top-of-the-line aircraft, missiles, tanks, and other equipment to Syria, significantly tightening the dependency relationship. The enhanced Soviet position in Syria portends a potentially serious threat to Turkey's security by virtue of its presence and influence on the latter's southern flank. It also limits U.S. and NATO control of the eastern Mediterranean by placing their ships within range of missile concentrations near the Syrian coast. Furthermore, the Soviet use of the port of Latakia provides an important facility for sustaining naval operations in the Mediterranean without having constantly to transit the Turkish Straits to reach home ports in the Black Sea.

The Soviet position in Syria might also be exploited by Moscow in its efforts to pressure Ankara into tolerating increased Soviet violations of the Montreux Convention limiting passage of warships through the Turkish Straits. Robert G. Weinland has written:

> It is worth noting in this regard that in July of 1976, as the new Soviet aircraft carrier KIEV left the Black Sea on its maiden voyage, the Soviet navy's professional journal *Morskoy Sbornik* published an article on the Montreux Convention that elicited wide attention in the West. That attention was focused on the assertion that Black Sea powers were entitled to send any ship through the Turkish Straits—even aircraft carriers, ostensibly denied passage by the Convention. This article contained a second, only slightly less radical departure from the norm: the contention that the ships of Black Sea powers operating outside the Turkish Straits should be able to return to port if necessary without the eight days' prior notice called for by the Convention. This argument attracted little attention. Its full implementation, however, could well open the Turkish straits to the degree that adequate support for the Soviet Mediterranean Squadron could in fact be provided from the Black Sea.[24]

Since the 1960s the Soviets have been actively engaged in a long-term strategy designed to neutralize Turkey in the event of a conflict between NATO and the Warsaw Pact. However, the Soviets have clearly expected to reap significant interim benefits from an improvement of bilateral relations. For one thing, such improved relations would preclude Turkey from allowing itself to be used as a forward base for NATO power projection against the Soviet Union. It would also give Moscow a freer hand in pursuing its ambitions in the Middle East, provided that they could be carried out in a way that was not perceived in Ankara as a potential threat to Turkish security. The Middle East might even be turned into a nuclear-free zone, giving the Soviets a regional monopoly in nuclear weapons. Turkish support of the idea of transforming the Mediterranean into a ''zone of peace'' would also have the benefit of making U.S. fleet visits to Turkish ports politically sensitive and ultimately unnecessary and probably unwelcome. Improved economic ties would reduce Turkey's dependence on the West and demonstrate that it could assert its independence in its foreign relations without fear of the consequences of possibly losing U.S. and NATO aid. To some extent, Moscow has been successful in reducing the probability of Turkey's participation in a NATO–Warsaw Pact conflict that did not pose a direct threat to Turkish interests. Duygu B. Sezer noted:

Turkey's desire to reassure the Soviet Union of her nonoffensive intentions has been a consistent element in her approach to major security-related issues and choices since the mid–1960s. The Declaration of the Principles of Good Neighbourliness, signed in April 1972 in Ankara, and the Political Document on the Principles of Good Neighbourly and Friendly Co-operation, drafted in 1975 and signed in June 1978 in Moscow, have come to stand as proof that the level of mutual confidence achieved so far allows for political as well as economic contacts. . . . Nearly fifteen years of official contacts, technical assistance and the absence of intimidation led Prime Minister Ecevit to declare, on 15 May 1978 in London, that the Soviet Union was not a threat to Turkey.[25]

The current position of Ankara on security matters appears to be that Turkey will adhere to the alliances with the United States and NATO for defensive purposes. However, it will not allow its territory to be used in a way that could reasonably be interpreted as posing a possible threat to Soviet security. As has been suggested, this represents a substantial achievement for Soviet policy and enhances Moscow's freedom of action in actively pursuing its strategic aims in the Middle East.

In the Red Sea region, the Soviets have nurtured a close relationship with the People's Democratic Republic of Yemen (PDRY) since it became independent in 1969. In October 1979, the two states entered into a 20-year treaty of friendship and cooperation, which, in effect, put the PDRY in the same category as Cuba and Vietnam. The Soviets have received permission for the liberal use of facilities at the former British naval base at Aden and at Socotra Island in the Arabian Sea. Such permission constitutes a de facto concession of the bases to the Soviet Union, notwithstanding the legal fiction that such bases do not exist because they have not been so designated de jure. From its position in the PDRY, coupled with its access to facilities in Ethiopia, the Soviet Union exercises de facto control of the southern end of the Red Sea.

In the central Mediterranean, Soviet links to the island nation of Malta provide Moscow with an additional point from which to contest U.S. and NATO dominance of the critical waterway. In 1981, Malta signed a neutrality agreement with the Soviet Union under which, in the event of a threat to international peace, Malta would consult with Moscow ''in order to adopt a common attitude.'' Subsequently, the Soviets received limited repair privileges for merchant ships and the right to store 200,000 tons of diesel fuel to service 200 ships annually at Maltese ports that had previously been reserved exclusively for the vessels of NATO members. In addition, the Soviets have established important economic links with the tiny country that serve to further secure their position there. Under a recent agreement, Malta will construct eight 8,500-ton ships for the Soviets, the largest vessels ever built in Maltese shipyards.[26] According to a report published in France, Malta ''has become a support base for the Soviets. . . . The Soviet objective is to turn Malta into a Cuba of the Mediterranean.''[27]

The Coasts of Africa

Around the periphery of Africa, Soviet bases, facilities, and anchorages can be found along the vital cape route connecting the Atlantic and Indian oceans. From Cape Verde off the west coast of Africa to Socotra Island in the Arabian Sea off the Horn of Africa, the Soviets have been attempting to build a chain of forward positions from which they might challenge Western control of the sea route that is critical not only to NATO but also to the Soviet Union itself.

The Cape Verde Islands, a group of 18 small islands off the coast of West Africa, are located astride the major coastal sea lanes and serve as an Atlantic gateway for the cape route around Africa. According to a leader of the opposition to the Marxist government of the islands, Soviet engineers are building a naval base and submarine pens in a protected natural deep-water harbor. In addition, the islands are reportedly being used as a transfer depot for Eastern bloc ships and planes transiting the region.[28]

A key target for the Soviet Union is South Africa, primarily because of its control of the strategically important Cape of Good Hope. The significance of the cape has been recognized by the maritime states of the West for more than 200 years. As Lord Castlereagh wrote to Corn-wallis, the governor-general of India, in 1805, "the true value of the Cape to Great Britain is its being considered and treated at all times as an outpost subservient to the protection and security of our Indian possessions . . . its occupation is perhaps even more material as depriving the enemy of the best intermediary position between Europe and India."[29]

It seems quite clear that the Soviets have also long regarded South Africa as a major strategic prize, notwithstanding that many in the West today tend to downgrade its strategic importance, primarily, it would appear, in order to avoid the necessity of dealing with its government.[30] Soviet writers have tended to focus on the obvious facts that South Africa straddles the meeting point of the Atlantic and Indian oceans, and that the sea lanes following the cape route must of necessity come close to its shores. One Soviet commentator notes that "the 'loss' of South Africa would deprive the multinational monopolies and their global strategy-makers of an important military and political outpost at the junction of the Indian and Atlantic Oceans."[31] Another is even more explicit in arguing that South Africa occupies "key positions at the junction of the Indian and Atlantic Oceans, controlling the sea routes around the southern extremity of Africa." He also notes that some 75 percent of the oil of the Persian Gulf and 44 percent of the freight trade of the NATO countries traverse these routes. He concludes by arguing that "the strategic role of RSA has grown especially after the fall of Portugal's colonial empire in Africa which deprived the Western powers of very important bases on the African continent."[32]

The Soviets are keenly aware that the major naval base at Simons-town, notwithstanding the current refusal of the United States and other Western powers to make use of it because of political differences with the South African government over its racial policies, continues to remain a strategic asset of incalculable importance for the control of the cape route. As Sir Robert Thompson has observed, the loss of Western control over the cape route, and with it the Indian Ocean, "would cut the world vertically in half and give Russia complete hegemony, except for China, over the three main land continents of Europe, Asia, and Africa."[33] That the present course of events may indeed lead to such dire consequences is clearly reflected in the argument of Robert J. Hanks, who cautions: "It should not be overlooked that, with the fall of Angola and Mozambique to Marxist forces, some five thousand miles of the Cape Route are now bereft of any port or airfield from which Western naval and air forces can operate—or receive support—in routine peacetime or far more demanding wartime circumstances. Self-imposed Western denial of access to Simonstown—as well as to other South African ports, Durban and Richards Bay especially—has, in effect, forfeited this portion of the Cape Route to the Soviet Union. The implications of this change in the strategic equation hardly need elaboration.''[34]

A 20-year treaty of friendship and cooperation was signed with the Marxist government of Mozambique on March 31, 1977. The treaty contains a provision that ''in case of situations tending to threaten or disturb the peace,'' the two states ''will immediately contact one another with the aim of coordinating their positions in the interest of eliminating the threat or reestablishing peace.'' Another clause states that the two countries will continue to cooperate in the military sphere on the basis of existing security agreements between them.[35] In regard to the latter provision, the Soviet Union has received permission to make use of the Mozambican ports of Maputo and Nacala. From these points the Soviets are in a position to exercise virtual control of the sea lanes through the passage between Madagascar and the African continent.

The Soviets currently also have access rights in the Indian Ocean island nations of Reunion, Comoro, and Mauritius and an anchorage in the Seychelles.[36] With regard to the last of these, Miytaba Razvi suggests that ''the Russians see the Seychelles as strategically located and feel the island can be effectively used to balance the US naval base of Diego Garcia.''[37]

The Soviet Union is at present well established in Ethiopia, where, since the late 1970s, it has had access to port facilities at Assab and Massawa, as well as the Dahlak Islands in the Red Sea. The Soviets have also constructed a military airfield on Dahlak from which they can control much of the region. The Soviet position in Ethiopia was achieved as a consequence of the strategically motivated abandonment of their long-standing base in Somalia. Here again, the Soviets took advantage of an opportunity that was created for them by others. As described by Robert Aliboni, ''the USSR had no grand design, perhaps no design at all; it exploited the opportunities offered by the situation as well as it could, ironically transforming a policy intended to weaken it and eliminate it from the region, into a reinforcement of its presence in the region.''[38]

Notwithstanding the loss of the heavy Soviet investment in developing the base at Berbera in Somalia, Ethiopia, from a strategic perspective, is by far the more important prize because of its position in Africa relative to Sudan and Egypt. Ethiopia contains the source of the Blue Nile, a position that gives it, and presumably the Soviets as well, the ability to apply potentially powerful geopolitical leverage on Egypt and Sudan, which are both critically dependent on its waters. Also, as was suggested earlier, Soviet de facto bases in Ethiopia, coupled with comparable facilities in South Yemen, assure the ability to exercise full control of the Bab al-Mandab Strait and the southern Red Sea region, as well as the important international sea routes passing through them.

Finally, it is also of some significance that the Soviet Union has been using military assistance to expand its influence around the periphery of Africa. Though it is difficult to draw precise correlations between arms deliveries and influence leading to access to facilities, the Soviets have made a point of using military assistance as the primary means of penetration where other options are not readily available. It is worth noting that since 1980, 12 African littoral states have received more than half of their military equipment from the Soviet Union. These include Libya, Algeria, Cape Verde, Guinea Bissau, Benin, Equatorial Guinea, Congo, Angola, Mozambique, Madagascar, Tanzania, and Ethiopia.[39]

Southeast Asia

In Indochina, close to the Strait of Malacca, the Soviets took advantage of the latent hostility between the Chinese and the Vietnamese to develop a toehold in the strategically important country as early as 1965. Although North Vietnam was, as a practical matter, within China's orbit of influence, events of that year brought about a significant change in political alignments. With the onset of the U.S. air war against North Vietnam, Hanoi made a fundamental change in its war strategy that provided an opening for Moscow to replace China as its major ally and patron. The new North Vietnamese strategy involved a switch from the Mao model of protracted guerrilla warfare to the Giap model of compressed warfare. The shift from guerrilla war to positional war meant a requirement for armor, aircraft, and air defense equipment that China could not provide but that the Soviet Union could and did.[40]

Though Moscow did not entirely replace Beijing as Hanoi's chief ally for some years, it had set the stage for the signing of the Soviet–Vietnamese treaty of friendship and cooperation in 1978. Since then there has been increased Soviet use of air and naval bases and facilities in Vietnam, Cambodia, and Laos, and Admiral Ronald Hays, commander-in-chief of the U.S. Pacific Command, considers the Soviet buildup at Cam Ranh Bay to be "the most significant development in this theater in recent years. When you look at it from a strategic sense, Cam Ranh Bay gives them the warm water port that they have been seeking since Catherine the Great."[41] Though this judgment is something of an overstatement, the significance of the Soviet buildup should not be minimized.

The precise numbers and types of Soviet forces at Cam Ranh Bay and other bases in Vietnam and Cambodia are now more difficult to assess as a consequence of the opening of a new air corridor from the Soviet Union across India, which is not under reliable surveillance. Nevertheless, recent intelligence reports indicate that between 20 and 25 Soviet naval vessels, including a handful of cruise missile and attack submarines, operate from the base at Cam Ranh Bay, which is also reportedly equipped with surface-to-air missile batteries to defend it against air attack. In addition, the base boasts at least a half-dozen floating docks, 3,000-meter runways, fuel storage tanks, and direction finder systems that can pinpoint ships operating in nearby waters. Soviet capabilities in southern Vietnam are presently considered by U.S. estimates to include some 16 Tu–16 (Badger) intermediate-range (1,500 n.m.) bombers, 8 Tu–95 (Bear D/F) long-range (4,500 n.m.) reconnaissance and antisubmarine warfare aircraft, and a squadron of MiG–23 (Flogger) fighter planes.[42] In the view of the U.S. navy's chief of intelligence, Rear Admiral John L. Butts, "Cam Ranh Bay now accommodates the largest concentration of Soviet naval assets outside the Soviet Union and, given the infrastructure improvements underway, an increase in the size of the presence is likely in the offing."[43]

Though these forces are outclassed at the moment by U.S. forces operating out of bases in the Philippines and thus pose no immediate threat to the security of the region, they nonetheless provide Moscow with the means of applying considerable political pressure on the regional states. According to the U.S. Pacific Fleet commander, Admiral James A. Lyons, Soviet bombers have been staging mock attacks in the direction of the Philippines. Since the United States has major military bases in the islands, these exercises are intended by Moscow to send a clear message to the Aquino government that the U.S. military presence will invite rather than deter attacks on the Philippines in the event of war between the United States and the Soviet Union.[44]

However, should the United States be requested by the Aquino government to withdraw from or significantly reduce its naval and air forces in the Philippines, the Soviet Union would become by default the dominant military power in the region. It would become the only major power strategically positioned to control the freedom of navigation along the vital sea lanes passing through the waters of Southeast Asia. This would have a considerable impact on China, for which the Soviet navy represents a significant offensive naval threat. Soviet submarines, operating without effective restraints, would be free to disrupt China's maritime commerce seriously, even within the east China and South China seas. As argued by Donald C. Daniel, the Soviet Union would be in a position to "seize China's offshore islands, destroy China's oil-exploitation facilities over the continental shelf and, if it wishes to pay the price, cannot be prevented from operating surface ships immediately off China's coast, using them to shell the mainland or to land amphibious forces."[45]

An unhindered Soviet capacity to interdict or delay selected shipping through the region would pose a major threat to the economic security of states as far away as Japan and South Korea. These highly industrialized countries are critically dependent on the freedom of passage through these sea lanes for vessels delivering oil from the Persian Gulf and minerals from Africa. Both would see a U.S. withdrawal from the Philippines as disastrous to their interests, subjecting them, particularly Japan, to pressures from the Soviet Union to sever their bilateral security treaties with the United States.

Finally, it is important to note that Vietnam, the Soviet Union's regional ally and client, has the largest military force in Southeast Asia and the third or fourth largest in the world. Furthermore, there is the distinct possibility that the Vietnamese themselves may begin to acquire the naval and air capability to project military power beyond Indochina. Since Vietnam is critically dependent on the Soviet Union for its military equipment and supplies, it is quite reasonable to assume that the Vietnamese armed forces may become available to act as Soviet surrogates in the region.[46]

Northeast Asia

In Northeast Asia, the long-standing Soviet relationship with North Korea has taken on significant new dimensions since the May 1984 visit of Kim Il-Sung to Moscow. In an apparent exchange for new supplies of sophisticated aircraft and missile systems, Moscow has received military overflight rights, giving it a new air corridor to Vietnam that avoids airspace under control of Japan and the United States. More significantly, the Soviets have gained increased naval access to North Korean bases in the Sea of Japan as far south as Wonsan, close to the South Korean border. Of particular concern are the increased visits and stopovers of Soviet naval vessels at Nampo, North Korea's main port and naval base in the Korea Gulf, which can be reached directly by overland route from Vladivostok.[47] A Soviet naval base on Korea's west coast would allow Moscow to bypass entirely the strategic choke points controlling access to and from the Sea of Japan and provide unimpeded access through the Yellow Sea to the China seas and the sea lanes of Asia.

This would in effect constitute a breakout from the confines of the stranglehold that could be applied against Soviet shipping in the Sea of Japan by U.S. and Japanese forces acting in concert in the event of crisis. It also poses a direct threat to China by placing the Soviet fleet in close proximity to Tsingtao, once home port of the U.S. Seventh Fleet and now a major Chinese naval base, and in a position to blockade Manchurian ports in the event of a hostile flare-up in Sino-Soviet relations. Finally, the Soviets have pursued a significant military buildup in the occupied northern islands, raising to 30 the number of Soviet air bases directly confronting Japan. These forces, as in the case of the Philippines, enhance Moscow's ability to intimidate the Japanese into a more accommodating political posture by making it clear that in the event of a Soviet-U.S. conflict, the U.S. bases in Japan will serve as a magnet drawing attacks against it.

Furthermore, in considering the import of the Soviet buildup in the region, perhaps not enough attention has been given to the possibility that Moscow may be seeking to lay the basis for a military capability that will allow it to strike decisively at U.S. bases and forces in the Western Pacific. The character of the Soviet buildup since 1978 appears to be placing ever greater emphasis on power projection capabilities. The positioning of more than one-third of the Soviet SS–20 mobile missile force in the Far East, as well as the addition of Backfire bombers into the Pacific Ocean Fleet Air Force, significantly increases Moscow's strategic and maritime strike capabilities in the broader region.[48] As Martin L. Lasater notes, "Soviet military strategy appears to emphasize increasingly the ability to move offensive forces into the open waters and air space of the Pacific in ways to avoid the strong US-Japanese air and sea defenses around the Japanese home islands."[49] Soviet sea and air access from and over North Korea may be intended in part to serve this larger strategic purpose. Evaluating the Soviet position in the region, the U.S. Pacific commander, Admiral Ronald J. Hays stated:

The Soviets, I think, have discovered the Pacific in the last two to three years, and since that realization, the Pacific is growing in importance not only for them but for the rest of the world, in particular the United States. They have brought in the finest military hardware they have, the new classes of ships, the MiG–31s and Backfires, and they have brought in additional helicopters and tanks to improve the mobility of their land forces. As a result, the Soviet military in the Pacific is no longer a home defense force, but rather a force that has capability of interdicting sea lines vital to us in such areas as the Aleutians and Alaska, Guam, Okinawa and even the mainland United States.[50]

A comparable assessment was made by James A. Kelly, on behalf of the Department of Defense, in testimony before the U.S. Congress on October 19, 1983.

The dramatic increase of Soviet offensive power in Asia and in the Pacific and Indian Oceans is the most far-reaching military development of recent years. . . . Soviet military forces in the Pacific for the first time pose a significant, direct conventional threat to U.S. forces, territory and lines of communication. We can no longer assume that an Asian conflict will be confined "over there" and that our involvement will be determined by whether we want to be involved or not. The Soviets now have and are steadily improving the capability to bring war to us by attacking our forward-deployed forces, our supply lines—including the critical Alaskan oil shipping lanes—and our territory in Guam and the Aleutians.[51]

Finally, Harry Gelman has pointed out that the geopolitical implications of the Soviet buildup in Northeast Asia reach far beyond the region.

In sum, the Soviet buildup in the Far East has evolved from relatively simple beginnings to more and more complex purposes. It increasingly defends not only the Soviet version of borders with China and Japan, but also a steadily widening circle of Soviet geopolitical interests elsewhere. The troops and weapons deployed against China have come to embody pressure on the PRC not only to accept the status quo on the Sino-Soviet frontier, but also to accept a new status quo more recently imposed in Indochina that is a fresh challenge to Chinese interests. Similarly, the Soviet planes and ships dispatched to the Far East not only challenge the Japanese and American position in the area, but assist Soviet prospects in Southwest Asia by exerting pressure on American military resource allocations.[52]

With limited assets available for deployment, the United States would be faced with a very difficult political dilemma. If, notwithstanding the escalating Soviet power there, it elected to reduce its presence in Northeast Asia in order to meet a crisis in the western Indian Ocean region, the effects on its bilateral alliance with Japan could be devastating. On the other hand, failure to do so could result in according the Soviets a free hand in a region of vital importance to both the United States and the Soviet Union. Given the increased Soviet dependence on the extremely long southern sea route, susceptible to interdiction at innumerable points along its passage, Moscow must place an ever greater premium on finding a way to reduce such vulnerability. And, indeed, the solution to this geostrategic problem appears to lie in Southwest Asia.

Notes

1. W. F. Bringle, "The Challenge Proposed by the Soviet Navy," *Journal of the Royal United Services Institute for Defence Studies*, June 1973, pp. 11–12.

2. V. Kudryavtsev, "The Indian Ocean in the Plans of Imperialism," *International Affairs* (Moscow), November 1974, p. 117.

3. *Izvestia*, January 17, 1980.

4. Albert E. Graham, "Soviet Strategy and Policy in the Indian Ocean," in Paul J. Murphy, ed., *Naval Power in Soviet Policy*, p. 284.

5. Cited by Albert L. Weeks, "Andropov Navalism," *Defense Science 2001 +*, April 1983, p. 16.

6. "Fresh Course for the Navy in a Changing World," *U.S. News and World Report*, October 20, 1975, p. 62.

7. Cited by Anthony H. Cordesman, "The Western Naval Threat to Soviet Military Dominance: A *Soviet* Assessment," *Armed Forces Journal Interna-*

tional, April 1983. (Reprinted in part in U.S. Department of Defense, *Current News: Special Edition*, no. 996, May 3, 1983, p. 12.)

8. Jack V. Roome, "Soviet Military Expansion in the Pacific," *Pacific Defence Reporter*, August 1986, p. 14.

9. Albert L. Weeks, "Soviet Navy's Huge Pacific Buildup Belies Moscow's Calls for Peace, Arms Reductions," *New York City Tribune*, September 8, 1986.

10. *Christian Science Monitor*, May 27, 1968.

11. Anne Kelly Calhoun and Charles Petersen, "Changes in Soviet Naval Policy: Prospects for Arms Limitations in the Mediterranean and Indian Ocean," in Paul J. Murphy, ed., *Naval Power in Soviet Policy*, pp. 237–38.

12. Walter Laqueur, *The Struggle for the Middle East*, p. 156.

13. *Pravda*, June 12, 1971.

14. Calhoun and Petersen, op. cit., p. 238.

15. FBIS, *Daily Report: Middle East and North Africa*, April 23, 1974.

16. FBIS, *Daily Report: Soviet Union*, July 22, 1974.

17. *Pravda*, September 9, 1974.

18. "Cairo Paper Says Libya Gives Soviet Military Facilities," *New York Times*, May 23, 1975; Charles Corddry, "Libya Reportedly Readies Pens for up to Six Soviet Submarines," *Baltimore Sun*, June 30, 1975.

19. Malcolm W. Browne, "Yugoslav Dockyards Repair Soviet Ships," *New York Times*, February 7, 1977.

20. Karen Dawisha, "The Correlation of Forces and Soviet Policy," in Adeed and Karen Dawisha, eds., *The Soviet Union in the Middle East*, p. 157.

21. Yosef Bodansky, "Soviet Military Presence in Libya," *Armed Forces Journal International*, November 1980, p. 89.

22. *Guardian*, February 25, 1983.

23. *Pravda*, March 18, 1983.

24. Robert G. Weinland, "Egypt and Support for the Soviet Mediterranean Squadron," in Paul J. Murphy, ed., *Naval Power in Soviet Policy*, p. 271, n. 40.

25. Duygu Bazoglu Sezer, "Turkey's Security Policies," in Jonathan Alford, ed., *Greece and Turkey: Adversity in Alliance*, p. 75.

26. *Washington Times*, December 24, 1984.

27. *Valeurs Actuelles*, December 3, 1984.

28. Gudrun Hassinen, "Soviets, Cubans Acting to Tighten Grip on Strategic Cape Verde Islands," *New York City Tribune*, October 6, 1986.

29. Cited by G. S. Graham, *The Politics of Naval Supremacy*, p. 40.

30. Morris Rothenberg, *The USSR and Africa: New Dimensions of Soviet Global Power*, pp. 222ff.

31. Dmitri Volsky, cited in Rothenberg, op. cit., p. 222.

32. I. A. Ulanovskaia, cited in Rothenberg, op. cit., p. 222.

33. Sir Robert Thompson, ''The Cost of Credibility,'' *New Lugano Review*, no. 8–9, 1976, p. 11.

34. Robert J. Hanks, *The Cape Route: Imperiled Western Lifeline*, p. 56.

35. David B. Ottaway, ''Soviet Pact Shores Up Mozambique,'' *Washington Post*, April 4, 1977.

36. Aryeh Yodfat and M. Abir, *In the Direction of the Gulf: The Soviet Union and the Persian Gulf*, p. 118.

37. Miytaba Razvi, ''Pakistan's Geopolitical Environment and Security,'' *Pakistan Horizon*, Third Quarter, 1982, p. 31.

38. Roberto Aliboni, *The Red Sea Region*, p. 73.

39. Richard B. Remnek, ''Soviet Military Interests in Africa,'' *Orbis*, Spring 1984, p. 142.

40. C. M. Noor Arshad, ''Southeast Asia in Soviet Perspective,'' *Asian Defence Journal*, May 1985, p. 40.

41. Cited by William Branigin, ''Soviet Military Operations Seen Increasing in the Pacific,'' *Washington Post*, August 1, 1986.

42. Ibid.

43. Cited by G. Jacobs, ''Soviet Pacific Fleet,'' *Combat Weapons*, Summer 1986, pp. 52ff.

44. Bernard E. Trainor, ''Russians in Vietnam: U.S. Sees a Threat,'' *New York Times*, March 1, 1987.

45. Donald C. Daniel, ''Sino-Soviet Relations in Naval Perspective,'' *Orbis*, Winter 1981, p. 797.

46. Jack V. Roome, ''Soviet Military Expansion in the Pacific,'' *Pacific Defence Reporter*, August 1986, p. 14.

47. Takio Yamazaki, ''The Soviet March toward Open Sea,'' *Survival in the 21st Century*, April 1986, p. 5; Edward Neilan, ''Soviet Naval Moves Annoy the Chinese,'' *Washington Times*, August 7, 1986.

48. Larry A. Niksch, ''Developments in Southeast Asia and Implications for US Interest,'' *Asian Defence Journal*, Novoember 1986, p. 31.

49. Martin L. Lasater, ''Moscow Steams Full Speed into America's Pacific Lake,'' *Asian Studies Center Backgrounder*, October 7, 1986, p. 3; Roome, op. cit., p. 12.

50. ''Soviet Shadow Is Apparent in Pacific Security Setting,'' *San Diego Union*, August 10, 1986. See also Drew Middleton, ''Soviet Expansion in Pacific, Far East Disquieting,'' *Defense News*, August 11, 1986.

51. James A. Kelly, ''Soviet Threat in Asia,'' *Retired Officer*, September 1984, p. 19.

52. Harry Gelman, *The Soviet Far East Buildup and Risk-Taking against China*, p. 109.

8   Expansion toward the Indian Ocean

For more than a century, Russian strategists have aspired to a warm-water outlet into the Indian Ocean. In the late nineteenth century it was seen as a prerequisite for capturing a fair share of the trade with India and the Orient, thereby creating markets essential to the commercial and industrial development of Central Asia. This aspiration is considered by many in the West today as a cliché, as a notion that no longer has any relevance in the context of contemporary international realities. This view, however, seems to reflect an unwillingness to confront the reality of an unrelenting Soviet drive for expansion and absolute hemispheric preponderance in Eurasia as a continuing motivation of Moscow's foreign and military policies. Breaking through the northern tier barrier is important precisely because it will allow the Soviets to establish a presence in the Persian Gulf and Middle Eastern area, and from there to project their power throughout the hemisphere. Indeed, because the Persian Gulf area is a land bridge to Africa and the Indian Ocean basin, establishing a secure foothold there is critical to the overall improvement of the Soviet global strategic posture. Hence, irrespective of its vast oil resources, the geopolitical centrality of the region was bound to foster intense Soviet interest in establishing a meaningful presence there. The Soviet Union aspires, at a minimum, to the kind of preeminence or arbiter status that Britain once enjoyed in the area. Sitting astride this strategic passageway would significantly enhance Soviet power projection capabilities and help impede or check those of Moscow's adversaries.[1]

This ambition to break out into the Indian Ocean probably has greater strategic significance for Moscow today than at any time in Russian history. Were the Soviets able to shift a major portion of their east-west traffic onto railroads and highways running to and from Soviet Caucasia and Central Asia through Iran, or through Afghanistan and Baluchistan, to Indian Ocean ports, they would dramatically improve their strategic communications situation. Direct and secure overland access to the Indian Ocean would relieve them of the current need to depend almost entirely upon the willingness of the Western alliance to allow their ships to transit the numerous NATO-controlled choke points in Europe. It would also cut the length of the southern sea route almost in half, thereby effectively doubling their available ship tonnage.

Not only would such an access corridor improve the lines of communication to the Far East, but it would also contribute significantly to a shift in the hemispheric balance of power in favor of the Soviet Union. Gregory Copley observes:

> It would enable the USSR to cut off energy supplies from the Middle East to Western Europe and Japan, and to move physically and securely along the North African landmass to physically outflank European NATO. The southern flank—i.e., North Africa—was considered vital by the Germans and the Allies in World War II. It is the key to the control of the southern European landmass.
>
> A southward thrust becomes strategically critical as a war-winning strategy for the USSR, because it offers advantages in Europe, Asia and the Pacific. Without a southward strategy, the USSR is left with untenable exterior lines of communications and insufficient logistics to support its critical Asia-Pacific strategies.[2]

A breakthrough to the south in Southwest Asia would also greatly enhance the importance of the Soviet bases at Cam Ranh Bay and Danang in Vietnam, which would become the pivot of a possible Soviet line of control along the periphery of Asia anchored at the Iran-Baluchistan coast at one end and Petropavlovsk and Vladivostok at the other. It would pose a far more serious challenge to a U.S. naval and military presence in the Indian Ocean, which operate without significant forward bases in the area. It would seriously impair the freedom of action of both India and Pakistan, as well as China, in the South Asian region. Furthermore, it could pose a substantial threat to the security of the international sea lines of communication transiting the area. Recognizing Japan's and South Korea's economic dependence on the freedom of navigation along those maritime routes, the Soviets would be in a position to hold them hostage against accommodations elsewhere in Asia.

It is interesting that many Chinese analysts also tend to believe that Southwest Asia is the most likely target for Soviet expansion in the near future. This is predicated largely on the perception of the existence of an effective East-West stalemate in both Europe and Northeast Asia. The essence of the argument is that in neither region is the Soviet Union capable of achieving a decisive victory, notwithstanding its overall margin of military superiority. Thus, Hua Di argues:

> Advancing southward, where the United States does not have prestationed forward bases and thus will have to count on lines of communication prolonged and susceptible to interruption, the Red Army could make full use of its superior conventional land forces and its geographical advantages of maneuver within a secure interior in a one-to-one duel against the American army without other NATO countries and Japan directly involved. Once the Red Army reaches Gwadar at the northern coast of the Arabian Sea, the Soviet Union can readily control the vital oil supply and further stretch its power eastward to India and Indochina, westward to the Mediterranean coast opposite of Europe, and southward to sweep across Africa and, finally, subdue Japan and Western Europe without fighting destructive wars there.[3]

On the other hand, the same analyst goes on to suggest that if it is possible to contain the Soviets in South Asia, then the potential threat to both Europe and Northeast Asia, presumably including China, may never materialize.

The Soviet Union and Iran

There is an increasing Soviet presence and influence in Khomeini's Iran, notwithstanding the supposed ideological hostility between the two regimes and Moscow's occasionally overt support for Iraq. The Soviets have cultivated important friends among the top leadership of Iran, including President Ali Khamenei, Prime Minister Mir Hossein Mousavi, State Prosecutor-General Mousavi Khoeiniha, Minister of

Heavy Industry Behzad Nabavi, and Supreme Court Justice Abdul-karim Ardebili. All of these, who appear to have Khomeini's private support, are strong proponents of state control of the economy and thus find they have essential elements of secular ideological compatibility with the Soviet system.[4]

Furthermore, despite the virtual evisceration of the communist Tudeh party, which is now operating as an exiled opposition group in Afghanistan, Soviet inroads into the leadership circles of Iran reflèct a determination to pursue their strategic aims in the area even if it requires accommodation with ideological enemies in strictly communist terms. However, it would be premature to rule out the possibility of a successful post-Khomeini coup by the Tudeh, particularly if it formed a coalition with the much larger leftist Mujaheddin-i-Khalq. Presumably, if such a coup were to take place, Moscow would surely respond favorably to a request from such a friendly regime for assistance in securing the gains of its popular revolution. Under these circumstances, there can be little doubt that the Soviets would be granted base facilities in the gulf as well as on the ocean littoral, with direct rail access from the sea to the Soviet Union.

An alternative scenario for the realization of Soviet strategic aims in Iran rests on the fact that the country itself is not ethnically or religiously homogeneous. This suggests that, as is the case in Pakistan, there are opportunities for the dismemberment of Iran into a number of segments, several of which would be both strategically located and highly dependent on Soviet assistance. Of particular importance in this regard are the Azeris and the Kurds. The approximately eight million Azeris are closely related to their kinsmen across the border in Soviet Azerbaijan, with whom they have greater affinities than with the Persian majority in Iran. The Kurds, on the other hand, have long been actively struggling for an independent Kurdistan to be carved out of Iran, Iraq, and Turkey. The two and one-half million Iranian Kurds, who are Sunni Muslims, also have had long-standing connections with the Soviets and would be highly dependent on Soviet support in the event of a successful break from Iran in a period of post-Khomeini chaos. Since the Iranian government does not have firm control in Azerbaijan or Kurdistan, these areas have been increasingly susceptible to Soviet influence augmented by large numbers of Azeri and Kurdish communists returning from exile and sanctuary in the Soviet Union. There are estimates that, beginning about 1984, as many as 20,000 armed Soviet activists have crossed into Iran from Turkmenistan.[5]

It is quite conceivable that Moscow might elect to attempt a repetition of the events of 1945; that is, the proclamation of independent Azerbaijan and Kurdistan republics under the leadership of pro-Soviet communists. Predictably, the new governments would have to call upon the Soviet Union for economic and military aid, including military advisers. Thomas T. Hammond suggests that "over a period of time the numbers of such advisers could be increased to the point where Azerbaizhan and Kurdistan would be, in effect, under Soviet occupation. Moscow would then have control of provinces that contain a large part of the population of Iran, produce most of Iran's food, border on the crucial Shatt-al-Arab waterway, and are close to the oil fields of both Iran and Iraq. . . . The Azeris and the Kurds, for their part, would have no choice but to seek close ties with the Soviets, since nobody else would protect them from Iran and Iraq."[6]

As a consequence of the Soviet development of an inland waterway system, it is now possible to travel by fairly large multi-use ships from Murmansk to Leningrad to the Caspian Sea. This extensive canal system was developed initially to reduce dependence on external sea lines of communication, particularly the difficult northern sea route. The canal linking the White Sea to the Baltic was completed in 1932, the Moscow-Volga Canal in 1937, and the Volga-Don Canal to both the Black and Caspian seas in 1952.[7] There are also already existing railroad links between Soviet Caucasia and western Iran at Tabriz. Links are now being completed between Meshed in northeastern Iran and the Soviet border at Sarakhs, where the railroad connects with a spur of the Trans-Siberian in Central Asia. When completed, the necessary bilateral railroad infrastructure to meet Soviet needs would already be in place. A post-Khomeini Iranian accommodation with the Soviets could well produce the sought-after corridor to the Indian Ocean. Should such not develop, Moscow still has an alternative at hand.

India-Pakistan-Afghanistan: The New "Great Game"

Even the most cursory consideration of geographic and demographic factors would suggest that India will ultimately play the major geopolitical role in the Indian Ocean region, comparable to that of China in

East Asia. It was thus not long after India gained its independence that the Soviet Union began to cultivate its relationships with the successive regimes in New Delhi. It seems quite clear that, as early as the mid 1950s, the Kremlin anticipated possibly serious problems with the Chinese and began to seek alternative power relationships in Asia. India in particular, given its massive size and very large population, seemed like a good prospect for serving as a counterweight to China. Accordingly, Moscow began its overtures to India during the very period in which Sino-Soviet relations were at their peak.[8]

Moscow's outreach to New Delhi was inadvertently assisted by the United States as a consequence of its program of aid to Pakistan. The enhancement of Pakistan's military capabilities was seen by India less as a move to contain Soviet expansion to the south than as a threat to its own aspirations of becoming the preeminent power in the subcontinent. Nehru was therefore receptive to the Soviet overtures, which he saw as offsetting the U.S. intervention in the region. What Nehru had not anticipated was the emergence of the Sino-Soviet conflict and the effect it would have on India's relations with China. There is reason to believe that the deterioration in India's relations with China a few years later was in large measure a consequence of the Indo-Soviet relationship that was established in 1955.[9] India soon found itself confronted with a hostile Pakistan to the west and a newly hostile China to the north and east. New Delhi's quite understandable concern about having potential enemies on opposite flanks has served to strengthen its relationship with Moscow over the years as a means of offsetting its strategic liabilities. As argued by Leo E. Rose, since the early 1960s the Soviets have reaped geostrategic advantage from the "occasionally violent competition between Peking and New Delhi for a hegemonic position in this difficult frontier area. It is obviously in the interest of the Soviet containment-of-China policy to keep the Sino-Indian boundary a 'hot' border and to discourage any rapprochement. The Chinese have had to divert to Tibet substantial military and logistic resources from its disputed borders with the Soviet Union—not only to discourage any Indian military adventurism, but also to protect the vital communication system that runs through Tibet to China's exposed western province of Sinkiang."[10]

A Soviet-Indian naval assistance agreement was signed in 1965, and since then the Indian navy has been primarily Soviet supplied as well as Soviet trained. The Soviet-Indian connection advanced another step on August 9, 1971, when the two states signed a 20-year treaty of friendship and cooperation. This agreement appears to be nothing less than a de facto mutual defense treaty. Article 9 of the pact stipulates: "Each of the High Contracting Parties undertakes to refrain from giving any assistance to any third party taking part in an armed conflict with the other party. In case any of the parties is attacked or threatened with attack the High contracting Parties will immediately begin mutual consultations with a view to eliminating this threat and taking appropriate effective measures to ensure peace and security for their countries."[11]

Though initially little concern was expressed about this relatively benign-sounding agreement, suspicions were soon aroused that it may have had some more profound military implications. The admission by the Indian minister of foreign affairs on May 9, 1973 that "Soviet naval engineers" were present at the Vishkapatnam dockyard gave credence to the concern that the Soviets might receive use of the naval facilities there.[12] According to some sources, India had indeed promised to make port facilities available to the Soviets as part of the 1971 treaty.[13] India is reported also to have extended access for Soviet warships to facilities at Bombay, Cochin, Marmugao (Goa), and Port Blair in the Andaman Islands.[14] As recently as March 1984 the Indian Defence Ministry indicated that India and the Soviet Union had "a common perception" of international and regional threats to their security.[15]

The blossoming military relationship between Moscow and New Delhi appears to have produced some recent additional benefits of strategic significance for the Soviets. According to a report in the Japanese press, the Soviet Union has been granted an air corridor from the Tadzhik SSR across India and the Bay of Bengal (and apparently over Burma as well) to Vietnam.

Particularly noteworthy is the possibility that the Soviet Union is using the less conspicuous western route to further speed up its military buildup in Indochina. For instance, Japan's estimate of the Soviet air force power in Vietnam is "approximately 36 planes including 6 Tu–95 Bear bombers, 16 Tu–16 Badger bombers, and 14 MiG–23 fighters" . . . however, China has information that the total figure has increased to more than 50 . . . it is a matter of serious concern that intelligence gathering involving a region that poses a threat to the sea lanes linking Japan and the Middle East is becoming increasingly difficult.[16]

It is also expected that Moscow will have access to the air base at Arakonnam, which is reportedly being upgraded to accommodate the latest aircraft in the Soviet inventory.[17] There are also persistent reports that the Soviets have already received access to facilities at Vishka-patnam. It is also expected that they will be given base rights at the naval installation that the Soviets are helping to construct north of Sabang, in India's Nicobar Islands in the Andaman chain, near the entrance to the Strait of Malacca. The presence of Soviet submarines in the area has been confirmed.[18]

Another recent development suggests an even more aggressive Indian role in regional affairs, especially if the relationship with the Soviet Union continues to develop and solidify. Selig S. Harrison suggests that India has now evolved its own version of a "Monroe Doctrine" for the Indian Ocean region. "India sees itself as an emerging power and is determined to achieve a dominant position in South Asia commensurate with its overwhelming preponderance in population, resources, and economic strength. Although it does not object to commercial sales of military equipment per se to other countries of the region, India seeks to minimize sales of sophisticated equipment that would significantly affect its margin of military superiority and thus force it to boost military expenditures further to maintain what it considers an acceptable balance."[19]

In the fall of 1986, New Delhi announced the construction of a new major naval base at Karwar on India's west coast. As is indicated by an editorial in the New Delhi press, the location of the base

is meant to improve the Indian Navy's reach across the Arabian Sea in pursuit of . . . what is known in naval parlance as "sea control" or the denial of the sea to forces inimical to Indian interests . . .

Tactically, it enables the Indian Navy to deploy at short notice at the centre of the Arabian Sea and straddle the approaches from the Red Sea and the Indian Ocean to the Gulf and Pakistan. Given the fact that the U.S. has constructed a major air and naval base in Diego Garcia in mid–Indian Ocean and has acquired facilities in Kenya, Somalia, Egypt, Saudi Arabia, and Oman for its Rapid Deployment Force, reaction times for crisis management have been drastically reduced since 1971. These facilities enable the U.S. (and the French who are entrenched in the Reunion Islands and Djibouti) to interfere more quickly in crises on the Indian sub-continent. Afghanistan has been used by the West for the penetration of the Indian Ocean littoral and the Soviet Fleet has followed Western flotillas to prevent the situation from deteriorating.[20]

The implications of this perception are very serious. It would seem, if the editorial writer truly reflects the strategic thinking in New Delhi, that the major purpose of the new base is to allow Indian forces to be pre-positioned to interfere with the use by the Rapid Deployment Forces of the United States and its allies of the sea lanes between Africa and India in the event of crisis in the region. In other words, the Indian navy would be positioned to act as a regional Soviet surrogate in support of Moscow's plans for both Iran and Pakistan. Lending credence to this perception is the argument made by A. W. Grazebrook.

There has been a series of equipment and facilities decisions which indicate unmistakably that India is moving to add to her strong self-defence force a significant power projection capability . . . India has the ability to launch an attack on Sri Lanka, or to seize the Maldive Islands or the Seychelles, or to mount air, naval and limited land campaigns against (say) Malaysia or Indonesia.

The reason for India's acquisition of this power projection capability remains a mystery. There have been suggestions that the capability gives it the ability to preserve peace in the Indian Ocean by threatening to join the USSR against a pressing United States or *vice versa*. However, commonality of equipment and training gives it a much greater potential for operations with the Russians rather than with the Americans.[21]

Despite the many negative political consequences the Soviets have suffered from their invasion of Afghanistan, they have also made substantial and, on balance, probably more than compensatory gains. They accomplished the immediate goal of replacing an unreliable communist regime with a more stable and compliant one. The move also prevented the possible overthrow of communism in the country, reflecting thereby the continuing validity of the Brezhnev Doctrine. It enhanced the security of the Soviet Central Asian frontier by keeping this southern neighbor out of the hands of anti-Soviet elements, imposing a stronger barrier against the influx of dangerous Islamic influences emanating from Iran.

The most significant gain, however, is the improvement in the Soviet geostrategic posture in the region. The use of Afghani airfields at Shindand and Kandahar places Soviet aircraft closer to the Strait of Hormuz and the Persian Gulf oil terminals. But perhaps even more important, the improved Soviet position reflects a historic change in the geopolitical configuration of the Indian subcontinent as a whole. Afghanistan no longer serves as the traditional buffer state between the Russian empire in Asia and the British Empire in India. The occupation of Afghanistan has placed Soviet forces at the Khyber Pass, leading directly into the heartland of Pakistan and India. This gives the Soviet Union unprecedented leverage not only over these two countries, but over Iran as well.

From Afghanistan the Soviets are in a position to realize their ambitions through Pakistan. The Soviet Union has for some time been cultivating dependency relationships with Baluch and Pushtu nationalist tribal leaders. Were Islamabad to be preoccupied simultaneously with renewed Indo-Pakistani tensions over Kashmir, a nationalist insurrection along its northwestern frontier with Afghanistan calling for an independent Pushtunistan, or a similar outbreak in the south, where pro-Soviet Baluch tribal leaders could easily be induced to declare independence from Pakistan with the understanding that they could then request Soviet guarantees of their security, there would be little that could be done to reverse such a fait accompli. Indeed, there is good reason to believe that such an invitation for the Soviet Union to intervene in Baluchistan would probably be widely supported by the nonaligned states championed by India with, as Milan Hauner puts it, "NATO-Europe as passive onlookers pursuing detente with the Soviet Union."[22] A close examination of events in that region will indicate that such a scenario is far from improbable should it serve Soviet purposes.

The Baluch of Pakistan mounted a bitter and extremely violent insurrection against the government of Pakistan between 1973 and 1977. After the insurrection was suppressed, many of the Baluch rebels fled to Afghanistan. Among these were members of the Marxist Baluchistan People's Liberation Front, who have been training and preparing for the day when they can return to Pakistan to begin a new drive for independence. In addition, there are about 100,000 or more Baluch who are natives of Afghanistan, and about another 15,000 who live in the Soviet Union. This means that the Soviets could organize and train a Baluch liberation army in Afghanistan or the Soviet Union and smuggle weapons and agents into both Pakistan and Iran to prepare the groundwork for a forthcoming national liberation struggle. Even though Baluch leaders tend to view the Soviet intervention in Afghanistan as a matter of serious concern in terms of any future relationship of their own with the Soviets, they nonetheless have no other viable source of external support. Recognizing this, they have displayed caution in their public reactions to Soviet behavior. This situation presents Moscow with the opportunity, when it is convenient for its purposes, to promote a Baluch rebellion, against Pakistan as well as against Iran, that would lead to a pro-Soviet independent Baluchistan. It is a reasonable assumption that the regime of such a newly fashioned state might be prepared to provide its Soviet sponsors with the Indian Ocean outlet they have aspired to for so long in exchange for security guarantees and economic support. An independent Baluchistan indebted to Moscow and dependent on Soviet support against Iran and Pakistan might readily accommodate a Soviet wish to build naval and air bases at the ports of Gwadar, Pasni, and Ormara.[23] Furthermore, if the Baluch-populated parts of Iran were to be included in a new Baluch state, the Soviets would probably be able to establish a base at Shah Bahar, about 250 miles from the Strait of Hormuz.

The factors that could trigger a Soviet resolve to play the Baluch card are complex and relate primarily to how the Soviets see things evolving in both Iran and Pakistan. In the past, the Soviets have preferred to seek cooperation from the established governments of the region and have thus given relatively little nurture to Baluch national aspirations. Selig S. Harrison has argued:

> Soviet policy-makers recognize that although Baluch nationalism is boiling, it is still at a relatively low boil. So long as it remains at a low boil, the USSR is likely to seek maximum flexibility in pursuing its broader diplomatic and political objectives in the region, especially if the prospects for increasing Soviet influence in Islamabad and Teheran appear favorable. Conversely, in a climate of growing Baluch discontent, the Soviet Union would be tempted to follow an adventurist course. The temptation would be enhanced if Moscow confronts an entrenched anti-Soviet theocracy in Teheran and if it writes off its hopes for detaching Islamabad from its military ties to Peking and Washington. Moscow can afford to bide its time in deciding whether to play the Baluch card so long as there is no movement toward political settlements between the Baluch and the central governments of Pakistan and Iran.[24]

The border between Pakistan and India has been the scene of repeated military buildups by both sides recently, aggravated by India's own problems in the Punjab with Sikh nationalism. Furthermore, Pakistan's movement toward a nuclear weapons capability has long been a matter of great concern to New Delhi, which sees it as a potential threat to Indian security. Indian leaders are convinced that Pakistan's acquisition of massive quantities of conventional weapons, supplemented by an emerging nuclear weapons capability, might dramatically alter the strategic balance in the subcontinent, which, to a great extent, is currently in India's favor. Furthermore, India apparently believes that China is secretly assisting Pakistan in its nuclear development. From India's standpoint, the possibility of having nuclear-armed and allied powers on both its eastern and western flanks poses a security dilemma of unprecedented dimensions.[25] This development has recently evoked a barely veiled threat from the Soviet Union that it was not prepared to accept a Pakistani nuclear weapons capability. The fact that, as a consequence of the Soviet de facto annexation of the Wakhan corridor, the Soviet Union now borders directly on Pakistan suggests the possibility of a direct intervention. However, given the political ramifications of such a move, it seems more likely that Moscow would prefer to use a surrogate for the purpose. India would seem to be the most promising candidate for the task. It is neither difficult nor far-fetched to postulate a scenario where the Soviets would encourage India to eliminate the Pakistani nuclear facilities by initiating an offensive across the northwestern frontier. In the process, India would once again be in a position to assert its territorial claims in Kashmir, but this time with a much enhanced Soviet-supplied arsenal of sophisticated weaponry. It has been observed by Selig S. Harrison, that "despite efforts to put Indo-Pakistani relations on a more stable basis—notably, the Zia–Rajiv Gandhi pledge not to attack each other's nuclear installations—it would be a mistake to underrate the danger of an explosion. Festering local conflicts in the unsettled border areas of Punjab, Kashmir, and Sind could quickly escalate into a larger conflagration in which the United States would once again find itself caught in the middle, as it did in 1965 and 1971.''[26] Indeed, in late January 1987, India placed its one-million man army on alert and sent large forces to the border with Pakistan. Four weeks later, on February 28, Prime Minister Gandhi announced an unprecedented 43 percent increase in the military budget for the following year, while freezing all other spending. Gandhi told the Indian parliament that although India was one of the world's poorest countries, it could not compromise its national security.[27]

Were such a clash with India to take place, Islamabad would have no choice but to shift virtually all of its military power to the north to meet the Indian challenge. This, in turn, would severely hamper Pakistan's ability to deal with uprisings in Pushtunistan and, especially, Baluchistan. The emergence of a Baluch national liberation regime, backed by Soviet forces, just across the border in Afghanistan, might well prove irreversible. Although not as useful from the Soviet standpoint as an access corridor to the Indian Ocean through Iran, a corridor through Afghanistan and then through Baluchistan from Quetta south to the ocean would nonetheless be a welcome alternative.

Continued Soviet domination of Afghanistan is therefore an important component of a broader strategy in Asia. Not only does it place Moscow in a position to achieve its long-standing ambition of access to the warm waters of the Indian Ocean, but it also provides the Soviet Union with control over the traditional westward route of conquest from Central Asia to the Middle East. This route, which is vulnerable to attack only from the south—that is, from maritime power projection—crosses Iran from east to west south of the Elburz Mountains. From Afghanistan the Soviets are well placed to protect that route against interference by an outside power.

Consequently, there is little reason to place any credibility in indications that the Soviet Union might seriously be interested in a settlement of the Afghanistan war on any terms other than would leave Moscow in a position to pursue its broader strategic objectives in Southwest Asia.

Given the growing strategic importance of a secure corridor from the Soviet Union to the Indian Ocean, coupled with the fact of the deployment of some 30 Soviet divisions north of the region between Turkey and Pakistan and the lack of any comparable countervailing U.S. capability in the area, there is good reason to believe that Southwest Asia will provide the venue for the next expansionist initiative by Moscow. However, by contrast with the Soviet intervention in Afghanistan, which had little immediate strategic impact, the next Soviet move in the region will probably directly affect the balance of power in Asia.

While it is imperative that the United States significantly enhance its capability to respond to crises in Southwest Asia, a strictly military response is not enough. The United States must take Soviet activities in the rimlands of Africa and most especially in Asia more seriously. It must pursue the political and economic initiatives required to inhibit Moscow's moves in the hemisphere to improve its overall geostrategic posture. The long-term peace and security of Asia and the Pacific Basin may come to depend on the ability of the United States and its allies to prevent Moscow from eliminating, or even significantly reducing, the current vulnerabilities of the Soviet Union's extended sea lines of communication to the Far East.

Notes

1. Dennis Ross, "Considering Soviet Threats to the Persian Gulf," *International Security*, Fall 1981, pp. 167–68.

2. Gregory Copley, "Why Moscow Looks to the South," *Defense and Foreign Affairs*, February 1985, p. 14.

3. Hua Di, "The Soviet Threat to the Northern Pacific Region from an Overall Point of View," *Atlantic Community Quarterly*, Spring 1986, pp. 29–30.

4. Shahrough Akhavi, "Let's Stop Worrying about the Soviet Threat to Iran," *Washington Post*, March 22, 1987.

5. Copley, op. cit., p. 14.

6. Thomas T. Hammond, *Red Flag over Afghanistan*, pp. 207–8.

7. David Fairhall, *Russia Looks to the Sea*, p. 59.

8. Bhabani Sen Gupta, "South Asia and the Great Powers," in William E. Griffith, ed., *The World and the Great Triangles*, p. 248.

9. Leo E. Rose, "The Superpowers in South Asia: A Geostrategic Analysis," *Orbis*, Summer 1978, p. 401.

10. Ibid., pp. 405–6.

11. Cited by Ferenc A. Vali, *Politics of the Indian Ocean Region*, p. 90.

12. B. Vivekanandan, "Naval Power in the Indian Ocean," *Round Table*, January 1975, p. 69.

13. Alvin Bernstein, "The Soviets in Cam Ranh Bay," *National Interest*, Spring 1986, p. 17.

14. W. A. C. Adie, *Oil, Politics, and Seapower: The Indian Ocean Vortex*, p. 46.

15. *International Herald Tribune*, March 10–11, 1984.

16. Akihiko Ushiba, *Sankei Shimbun* (Tokyo), June 23, 1986.

17. A. W. Grazebrook, "Flaws in US Navy's Pacific Philosophy," *Pacific Defence Reporter*, February 1986, p. 26.

18. BK151223 Hong Kong AFP in English, 12:14 GMT, 15 September 1986—Broadcast monitored and published by FBIS in *Daily Report: Asia and the Pacific*.

19. Selig S. Harrison, "Cut a Regional Deal," *Foreign Policy*, Spring 1986, p. 129.

20. "Strategic Karwar Base," *Patriot* (New Delhi), October 24, 1986.

21. A. W. Grazebrook, "India's Mounting Military Might," *Pacific Defence Reporter*, September 1986, pp. 18ff.

22. Milan Hauner, "Seizing the Third Parallel: Geopolitics and the Soviet Advance into Central Asia," *Orbis*, Spring 1985, p. 10.

23. Amaury de Riencourt, "India and Pakistan in the Shadow of Afghanistan," *Foreign Affairs*, Winter 1982/1983, p. 433.

24. Selig S. Harrison, *In Afghanistan's Shadow: Baluch Nationalism and Soviet Temptations*, p. 198.

25. T. V. Paul, "Will India Join the Nuclear Club?" *Peace Magazine*, August-September 1986, p. 22.

26. Harrison, "Cut a Regional Deal," pp. 128–29.

27. *New York Times*, March 1, 1987.

Bibliography

Adel, Daljit Sen. *China and Her Neighbours* (New Delhi, 1984).

Adie, W. A. C. *Oil, Politics, and Seapower: The Indian Ocean Vortex* (New York, 1975).

Alford, Jonathan, ed. *Greece and Turkey: Adversity in Alliance* (Aldershot, U.K., 1984).

Aliboni, Roberto. *The Red Sea Region* (London, 1985).

Arshad, C. M. Noor. "Southwest Asia in Soviet Perspective," *Asian Defence Journal*, May 1985.

Atkeson, Edward B. "The 'Fault Line' in the Warsaw Pact: Implications for NATO Strategy," *Orbis*, Spring 1986.

Auty, Robert, and Dmitri Oblensky. *An Introduction to Russian History* (London, 1976).

Azmi, M. Raziullah. "Russian Expansion in Central Asia and the Afghan Question (1865–85)," *Pakistan Horizon*, Third Quarter, 1984.

Beloff, Max. *The Foreign Policy of Soviet Russia*, 2 vols. (London, 1949).

Bernstein, Alvin. "The Soviets in Cam Ranh Bay," *National Interest*, Spring 1986.

Bhargava, G. S. *South Asian Security after Afghanistan* (Lexington, Mass., 1983).

Bodansky, Yosef. "Soviet Military Presence in Libya," *Armed Forces Journal International*, November 1980.

Braun, Dieter. "The USSR and South Asia: Long Term Strategies, Recent Activities," *Pakistan Horizon*, Fourth Quarter, 1984.

Bray, William G. *Russian Frontiers: From Muscovy to Khrushchev* (Indianapolis, 1963).

Bringle, W. F. "The Challenge Proposed by the Soviet Navy," *Journal of the Royal United Services Institute for Defence Studies*, June 1973.

Byrnes, James F. *Speaking Frankly* (New York, 1947).

Carpenter, Clifton C. "The Inner Asian Frontier: A Cradle of Conflict," *Strategic Review*, Winter 1977.

Chiang, Wego W. K. *The Strategic Significance of Taiwan* (Taipei, 1977).

Chew, Allen F. *An Atlas of Russian History* (New Haven, 1967).

Chubin, Shahram. *Security in the Persian Gulf: The Role of Outside Powers* (Totowa, N.J., 1982).

Churchill, Winston. *Triumph and Tragedy* (New York, 1953).

Clubb, O. Edmund. *China and Russia: The "Great Game"* (New York, 1971).

Clubb, O. Edmund. *Twentieth Century China* (New York, 1964).

Coates, W. P. and Zelda K. *Soviets in Central Asia* (New York: 1951).

Connolly, V. *Soviet Asia* (London, 1942).

Copley, Gregory. "Why Moscow Looks to the South," *Defense and Foreign Affairs*, February 1985.

Cordesman, Anthony H. "The Western Naval Threat to Soviet Military Dominance: A *Soviet* Assessment," *Armed Forces Journal International*, April 1983. (Reprinted in part in U.S. Department of Defense, *Current News: Special Edition*, no. 966, May 3, 1983.)

Cropsey, Seth. "Forward Defense or Maginot Line?" *Policy Review*, Fall 1986.

Curzon, George N. *Persia and the Persian Question* (London, 1892).

Curzon, George N. *Russia in Central Asia in 1889 and the Anglo-Russian Question* (London, 1889).

Daniel, Donald C. "Sino-Soviet Relations in Naval Perspective," *Orbis*, Winter 1981.

Dankewych, Michael. *Siberia in Global Power Politics: Economic, Strategic and Geographical Factors* (Washington, D.C., 1970).

Darius, Robert G., et al., eds. *Gulf Security into the 1980s: Perceptual and Strategic Dimensions* (Stanford, 1984).

Dawisha, Adeed and Karen, eds. *The Soviet Union in the Middle East* (New York, 1982).

Deluca, Anthony R. *Great Power Rivalry at the Turkish Straits: The Montreux Conference and Convention of 1936* (New York, 1981).

Di, Hua. "The Soviet Threat to the Northern Pacific Region from an Overall Point of View," *Atlantic Community Quarterly*, Spring 1986.

Dmytryshyn, Basil, ed. *Russia's Conquest of Siberia 1558–1700*, vol. 1, Documentary Record (Portland, Oregon, 1985).

Documents on International Affairs, 1936 (London, 1937).

Documents on International Affairs, 1953 (London, 1956).

Ebata, K. "The Second Siberian Railway," *Jane's Defence Weekly*, March 16, 1985.

Fairhall, David. *Russia Looks to the Sea* (London, 1971).

Fatemi, Faramarz S. *The U.S.S.R. in Iran* (South Brunswick, N.J., 1980).

Fischer, Louis. *Russia's Road from Peace to War* (New York, 1969).

Fischer, Louis. *The Soviets in World Affairs*, 2 vols. (Princeton, 1951).

Foucher, Michel. "Geopolitique de la question afghane," *Herodote*, October-December 1984.

Friters, G. M. "The Development of Outer Mongolian Independence," *Pacific Affairs*, September 1937.

Friters, G. M. "The Prelude to Outer Mongolian Independence," *Pacific Affairs*, June 1937.

Gallois, Pierre. "The Kola Peninsula and Its Strategic Importance," *Journal of Defense and Diplomacy*, September 1986.

Gelman, Harry. *The Soviet Far East Buildup and Risk-Taking against China* (Santa Monica, 1982).

Gilbert, Martin. *Atlas of Russian History* (Dorset House, 1985).

Gorbunov, V. "Our Dialogues: Building and Running the Baikal-Amur Mainline Railroad," *Socialist Industry*, January 15, 1985.

Graham, G. S. *The Politics of Naval Supremacy* (Cambridge, 1965).

Gray, Colin S. *The Geopolitics of the Nuclear Era* (New York, 1977).

Gray, Colin S. "Keeping the Soviets Landlocked: Geostrategy for a Maritime America," *National Interest*, Summer 1986.

Gray, Colin S. "Maritime Strategy and the Pacific: The Implications for NATO," *Naval War College Review*, Winter 1987.

Grazebrook, A. W. "Flaws in US Navy's Pacific Philosophy," *Pacific Defence Reporter*, February 1986.

Grazebrook, A. W. "India's Mounting Military Might," *Pacific Defence Reporter*, September 1986.

Griffith, William E., ed. *The World and the Great Triangles* (Cambridge, Mass., 1975).

Haberman, Clyde. "Challenge in the Pacific," *New York Times Magazine*, September 7, 1986.

Halliday, Fred. *Soviet Policy in the Arc of Crisis* (Washington, D.C., 1981).

Hammond, Thomas T. *Red Flag over Afghanistan* (Boulder, 1984).

Hamrin, Carol L. "China Reassesses the Superpowers," *Pacific Affairs*, Summer 1983.

Hanks, Robert J. *The Cape Route: Imperiled Western Lifeline* (Cambridge, Mass., 1981).

Hanks, Robert J. *The Pacific Far East: Endangered American Strategic Position* (Cambridge, Mass., 1981).

Harrison, Selig S. "Cut a Regional Deal," *Foreign Policy*, Spring 1986.

Harrison, Selig S. *In Afghanistan's Shadow: Baluch Nationalism and Soviet Temptations* (Washington, D.C., 1981).

Haselkorn, Avigdor. *The Evolution of Soviet Security Strategy 1965–1975* (New York, 1978).

Hauner, Milan. "Seizing the Third Parallel: Geopolitics and the Soviet Advance into Central Asia," *Orbis*, Spring 1985.

Hopkins, Joseph E., and William R. Warren. "Countering Soviet Imperialism," *Proceedings of the United States Naval Institute*, June 1979.

Hurewitz, J. C. *Diplomacy in the Near and Middle East: A Documentary Record, 1914–1956* (Princeton, 1956).

International Security Council. *The United States, China and the Soviet Union: Strategic Dilemmas and Options* (New York, 1968).

Ionescu, Ghita. *The Breakup of the Soviet Empire in Eastern Europe* (Baltimore, 1969).

Jackson, W. A. Douglas. *The Russo-Chinese Borderlands* (Princeton, 1968).

Jacobs, G. "The Soviet Navy in 1986: An Update," *Asian Defence Journal*, July 1986.

Jacobs, G. "Soviet Pacific Fleet," *Combat Weapons*, Summer 1986.

Johnson, A. Ross. "The Warsaw Pact: Soviet Military Policy in Eastern Europe," in Sarah M. Terry, ed., *Soviet Policy in Eastern Europe* (New Haven, 1984).

Jukes, Geoffrey. *The Soviet Union in Asia* (Berkeley: 1973).

Kapur, Harish. *Soviet Russia and Asia, 1917–1927: A Study of Soviet Policy towards Turkey, Iran and Afghanistan* (Geneva, 1966).

Kapur, Harish. *The Soviet Union and the Emerging Nations* (Geneva, 1972).

Kaushik, Devendra. *Soviet Relations with India and Pakistan* (Delhi, 1971).

Kazemzadeh Firuz. "Russia and the Middle East," in Ivo J. Lederer, ed., *Russian Foreign Policy: Essays in Historical Perspective* (New Haven, 1962).

Kelly, James A. "Soviet Threat in Asia," *Retired Officer*, September, 1984.

Kennan, George F. "The Sources of Soviet Conduct," *Foreign Affairs*, July 1947.

Kiernan, E. V. G. *British Diplomacy in China, 1880–1885* (Cambridge, 1939).

Kiliç, Altemur. *Turkey and the World* (Washington, D.C., 1959).

Klieman, Aaron S. *Soviet Russia and the Middle East* (Baltimore, 1970).

Ko Tun-hwa, and Yu-ming Shaw, eds. *Pacific Sealane Security: Tokyo Conference, 1983* (Taipei, 1984).

Ko Tun-hwa, and Yu-ming Shaw, eds. *Sea Lane Security in the Pacific Basin* (Taipei, 1983).

Krausse, Alexis. *Russia in Asia: A Record and a Study, 1558–1899* (New York, 1899).

Kudryavtsev, V. "The Indian Ocean in the Plans of Imperialism," *International Affairs* (Moscow), November 1974.

Kuniholm, Bruce R. *The Origins of the Cold War in the Near East* (Princeton, 1980).

Laqueur, Walter. *The Struggle for the Middle East* (New York, 1969).

Lasater, Martin L. "Moscow Steams Full Speed into America's Lake," *Asian Studies Center Backgrounder* (Washington, D.C.: Heritage Foundation), October 7, 1986.

Lederer, Ivo J., ed. *Russian Foreign Policy* (New Haven, 1962).

Lee, Robert H. G. *The Manchurian Frontier in Ch'ing History* (Cambridge, Mass., 1970).

Leighton, Marian. "Soviet Strategy Towards Northern Europe and Japan," *Survey*, Autumn-Winter 1983.

Lenczowski, George. *Russia and the West in Iran, 1918–1948* (New York, 1968).

Librach, Jan. *The Rise of the Soviet Empire* (New York, 1965).

Lobanov-Rostovski, A. *Russia and Asia* (New York, 1933).

Luttwak, Edward N. *The Grand Strategy of the Soviet Union* (New York, 1983).

Mansvetov, Fedor S. "Russia and China in Outer Mongolia," *Foreign Affairs*, October 1945.

Meissner, Boris. *The Brezhnev Doctrine* (Kansas City, 1970).

Menken, Jules. "Britain and the Persian Question," *National Review*, January 1946.

Middleton, Drew. "Soviet Expansion in Pacific Far East Disquieting," *Defense News*, August 11, 1986.

Mieczowski, Z. "The Soviet Far East: Problem Region of the USSR," *Pacific Affairs*, Summer 1968.

Millar, T. B., ed. *International Security in the Southeast Asian and Southwest Pacific Region* (Saint Lucia, Australia, 1983).

Mir Munshi, Sultan Mohammed Khan, ed. *The Life of Abdur Rahman, Amir of Afghanistan* (London, 1900).

Moore, Marc A. "Power Projection Strategy along East Asian Rimlands," *Marine Corps Gazette*, December 1986.

Morgenthau, Hans J. *Politics among Nations* (New York, 1949).

Morrison, Charles E., ed. *Threats to Security in East Asia-Pacific* (Lexington, Mass., 1983).

Munro, Neil. "Keeping Watch on the Amur and the Sea of Okhotsk," *Pacific Defence Reporter*, October 1986.

Murphy, Paul J., ed. *Naval Power in Soviet Policy* (Washington, D.C., 1978).

Niksch, Larry A. "Developments in Southeast Asia and Implications for US Interest," *Asian Defence Journal*, November 1986.

Nock, O. S. *World Atlas of Railways* (New York, 1978).

Nolde, Boris. *La formation de l'Empire Russe* (Paris, 1953).

Nollau, Guenther, and Hans J. Wiehe. *Russia's South Flank* (New York, 1963).

North, Robert N. "The Soviet Far East: New Centre of Attention in the U.S.S.R.," *Pacific Affairs*, Summer 1978.

O'Ballance, Edgar. "Gorbachev's Thoughts on China," *Asian Defence Journal*, October 1985.

Paul, T. V. "Will India Join the Nuclear Club?" *Peace Magazine*, August-September 1986.

Pierce, Richard A. *Russian Central Asia, 1867–1917* (Berkeley, 1960).

Pipes, Richard. *The Formation of the Soviet Union* (New York, 1974).

Ramazani, Rouhollah K. *The Northern Tier: Afghanistan, Iran, and Turkey* (New York, 1966).

Ranft, Bryan, and Geoffrey Till. *The Sea in Soviet Strategy* (Annapolis, 1983).

Rauch, Georg von. *A History of Soviet Russia* (New York, 1957).

Raymond, Ellsworth. "Mackinder's Prophecy: USSR Expansion," *Defense Science 2002 +* , June 1984.

Razvi, Miytaba. *The Frontiers of Pakistan* (Karachi, 1971).

Razvi, Miytaba. "Pakistan's Geopolitical Environment and Security," *Pakistan Horizon*, Third Quarter, 1982.

Remnek, Richard B. "Soviet Military Interests in Africa," *Orbis*, Spring 1984.

Rezun, Miron. *The Soviet Union and Iran* (Geneva, 1981).

Riencourt, Amaury de. "India and Pakistan in the Shadow of Afghanistan," *Foreign Affairs*, Winter 1982/1983.

Robinson, Thomas W. "Soviet Policy in Asia," *Problems of Communism*, November-December 1973.

Roome, Jack V. "Soviet Military Expansion in the Pacific," *Pacific Defence Reporter*, August 1986.

Rose, Leo E. "The Superpowers in South Asia: A Geostrategic Analysis," *Orbis*, Summer 1978.

Ross, Dennis. "Considering Soviet Threats to the Persian Gulf," *International Security*, Fall 1981.

Rostow, Eugene V. "Of Summitry and Grand Strategy," *Strategic Review*, Fall 1986.

Rothenberg, Morris. *The USSR and Africa: New Dimensions of Soviet Global Power* (Miami, 1980).

Routh, D. A. *Survey for 1936* (London, 1937).

Rywkin, Michael. *Russia in Central Asia* (New York, 1963).

Salisbury, Harrison E. *War between Russia and China* (New York, 1970).

Scherer, John L., ed. *USSR Facts and Figures Annual*, vol. 10 (Gulf Breeze, Fla., 1986).

Segal, Gerald, ed. *The Soviet Union in East Asia* (London, 1983).

Shabad, Theodore, and Victor L. Mote. *Gateway to Siberian Resources* (Washington, D.C., 1977).

Simes, Dmitri K. "Gorbachev: A New Foreign Policy?" *Foreign Affairs*, vol. 65, no. 3, 1987.

Singh, K. R. *Iran: Quest for Security* (New Delhi, 1980).

Solomon, Richard, and Masataka Kosaka, eds. *The Soviet Far East Military Buildup* (Dover, 1986).

Sontag, R. J., and J. S. Brodie, eds. *Nazi-Soviet Relations, 1939–1941: Documents from the Archives of the German Foreign Office* (Washington, D.C., 1948).

Spector, Ivan. *The Soviet Union and the Muslim World 1917–1958* (Seattle, 1959).

Stephenson, Graham. *Russia from 1812 to 1945* (New York, 1970).

Sumner, B. H. *Peter the Great and the Emergence of Russia* (New York, 1962).

Taafe, R. N., and R. C. Kingsbury. *An Atlas of Soviet Affairs* (New York, 1965).

Tang, Peter S. H. *Russian and Soviet Policy in Manchuria and Outer Mongolia, 1911–1931* (Durham, N.C., 1959).

Terry, Sarah M., ed. *Soviet Policy in Eastern Europe* (New Haven, 1984).

Thaden, Edward C. *Russia's Western Borderlands, 1710–1870* (Princeton, 1984).

Thompson, Sir Robert. "The Cost of Credibility," *New Lugano Review*, no. 8–9, 1976.

Thomson, Gladys S. *Catherine the Great and the Expansion of Russia* (New York, 1962).

Thornton, Richard C. "Strategic Change and American Foreign Policy: Perceptions of the Sino-Soviet Conflict," *Journal of Northeast Asian Studies*, Spring 1986.

Towle, Philip. *Naval Power in the Indian Ocean* (Canberra, 1979).

U.S. Department of State. *The Conferences at Malta and Yalta, 1945* (Washington, D.C., 1955).

U.S. Department of State. *The Problem of the Turkish Straits* (Washington, D.C., 1947).

U.S. Department of State. *Texts of the Russian "Peace"* (Washington, D.C., 1918).

U.S. Department of State. *Texts of the Ukrainian "Peace"* (Washington, D.C., 1918).

Vali, Ferenc A. *Bridge across the Bosporus* (Baltimore, 1971).

Vali, Ferenc A. *Politics of the Indian Ocean Region* (New York, 1976).

Vali, Ferenc A. *Rift and Revolt in Hungary* (Cambridge, Mass., 1961).

Vali, Ferenc A. *The Turkish Straits and NATO* (Stanford, 1972).

Vego, Milan. "The Soviet Envelopment Option on the Northern Flank," *Naval War College Review*, Autumn 1986.

Vernadsky, George. *A History of Russia* (New Haven, 1948).

Vivekanandan, B. "Naval Power in the Indian Ocean," *Round Table*, January 1975.

Voslensky, Michael. *Nomenklatura* (New York, 1984).

Walsh, Warren B. *Russia and the Soviet Union* (Ann Arbor, 1958).

Wandycz, Piotr S. *Soviet-Polish Relations 1917–1921* (Cambridge, Mass., 1969).

Warner, Denis. "The Bear across the China Border," *Pacific Defence Reporter*, September 1986.

Weeks, Albert L. "Andropov Navalism," *Defense Science 2001* + , April 1983.

Westwood, James T. "The Relentless March," *Army*, June 1981.

Westwood, James T. "The Soviet Union and the Southern Sea Route," *Naval War College Review*, January-February 1982.

Westwood, James T. "Japan and Soviet Power in the Pacific," *Strategic Review*, Fall 1983.

Westwood, James T. "Soviet Maritime Strategy and Transportation," *Naval War College Review*, November-December 1985.

Witte, Sergei I. *The Memoirs of Count Witte* (New York, 1921).

Yamazaki, Takio. "The Soviet March toward Open Sea," *Survival in the 21st Century*, April 1986.

Yodfat, Aryeh Y. *The Soviet Union and Revolutionary Iran* (London, 1984).

Yodfat, Aryeh Y., and M. Abir. *In the Direction of the Gulf: The Soviet Union and the Persian Gulf* (London, 1977).

Young, P. Lewis. "China and the South China Sea." *Asian Defence Journal*, July 1986.

Zagoria, Donald S., ed. *Soviet Policy in East Asia* (New Haven, 1982).

Index

About the Author

MARTIN SICKER earned his Ph.D. in political science from the Graduate faculty of the New School for Social Research in New York. He has served as a senior executive in the United States government, where he held a number of management and policy-level positions, and has taught political science at The American University and George Washington University in Washington, D.C. He has written widely in the fields of political science and international affairs and is the author of *The Making of a Pariah State: The Adventurist Politics of Muammar Qaddafi* and *The Judaic State: A Study in Rabbinic Political Theory*.

Dr. Sicker is now a private consultant and lecturer on international affairs and resides in Silver Spring, Maryland.